Cities

Symons, Arthur

BIBLIOLIFE

CITIES

BY

ARTHUR SYMONS

WITH EIGHT
PHOTOGRAVURES

1905
LONDON
J. M. DENT & CO.
New York: JAMES POTT & CO.

TO MADAME LA COMTESSE DE
LA TOUR

As you know, and, I sometimes think, regret, I am one of those for whom the visible world exists, very actively; and, for me, cities are like people, with souls and temperaments of their own, and it has always been one of my chief pleasures to associate with the souls and temperaments congenial to me among cities. And as love, or, it may be, hate, can alone reveal soul to soul, among human beings, so, it seems to me, the soul of a city will reveal itself only to those who love, or, perhaps, hate it, with a far-sighted emotion. I have come upon many cities which have left me indifferent, perhaps through some accident in my way of approach; at any rate, they had nothing to say to me: Madrid, for instance, and Vienna, and St Petersburg, and Berlin. It would be impossible for me to write about these cities: I should have nothing to say. But certain other cities, Rome, Venice, Seville, how I have loved them, what a delight it was to me merely to be alive, and living in them; and what a delight it is to me to think of them, to imagine myself in their streets and on their waters! Moscow, Naples, how I have hated them, how I have suffered in them, merely because I was there; and how clearly I see them still, with that sharp memory of discomfort! It seems to me that all these cities have given up to me at least something of their souls, like the people I have loved and hated on my way through the world. At least they have given me what they had to give me, like the people: my part of their souls. For we can see or receive, in people or things, only our own part of them: the vision rising in our own eyes, the passion rising in our own hearts.

This is not saying that I have not tried to do more than write a kind of subjective diary, in which the city should be an excuse for my own sensations. I have put myself as little as possible into these pages; I have tried to draw confidences out of the stones that I have trodden but a few weeks or a few months, out of the faces that I have seen in passing, out of the days of sunshine that have after all warmed a stranger. I have respected the sight of my eyes and the judgment of my senses, and I have tried to evoke my cities in these pages exactly as they appeared to me to be in themselves. It is part of my constant challenge to myself, in everything I write, to be content with nothing short of that *vraie vérité* which one imagines to exist somewhere on this side of ultimate attainment. It is so much easier to put oneself into things than to persuade things to give up their own secrets; and I like to aim at this difficult kind of truth.

What is truth? you will say: yes, the old question, which no one has ever answered. I am only explaining my intentions.

ARTHUR SYMONS.

CHÂTEAU DE CHAMÉANE,
PUY DE DÔME, *August* 1903.

CONTENTS

LIST OF ILLUSTRATIONS

ROME

ROME

I

THE last sunset of the year had been stormy; the whole sky, as I saw it from the Pincio, blazed like a conflagration; fire caught the farthest roofs of Rome, and seemed to sear the edges and outskirts of the city, like a great flame coming down from heaven. This flame burnt with an unslackening ardency long after the sun had gone down below the horizon; then the darkness began to creep about it, and it grew sombre, drooping into purple, withering into brown, dwindling into a dull violet, and from that wandering into a fainter and fainter greyness, until the roofs, jutting like abrupt shadows into the night, seemed to go up like smoke all round the city, as if the great fire were smouldering out. Darkness came on rapidly, there was no moon, and as I stood, just before midnight, by the side of the Forum, under the shadow of the Arch of Septimius Severus, I seemed at first to be standing at the edge of a great black abyss. Gradually, as I looked down, I became aware of a sort of rocky sea, a dark sea of white and slender rocks, which, as I watched them, seemed to heighten into the night. Near the triumphal arch I could distinguish the eight smooth columns of the Temple of Saturn; there, on the other side of this gulf, was the Palatine; and but a little to my left, though unseen, the Arch of Titus, and the Colosseum. In those imperishable ruins, which are still, after more than twenty centuries, the true Rome, the Rome which really exists, I saw the only human immortality which I had ever visibly seen. The twelve strokes of midnight, coming from the Christian churches on all sides, sounded faintly, as if they did but reckon the time of years, not of centuries. It was Pagan Rome that lasted, and Pagan Rome means humanity, working regardless of itself, and with the world at its feet, as a quarry to build from. This Rome, even in ruins, bows the mind before its strength, its purpose, its inflexible success. I had come to Rome, thinking that it was as the city of the Popes that I should see the Eternal City. I was filled only with a sense of the power of things earthly, the eternity of an art wholly the work of men's hands, as I turned away from the Forum, in those first moments of the new year. I looked back : the Arch of Septimius Severus stood up, white and gigantic, blotting out the sky.

The soul of Rome, as one gradually realises it, first, I think, and not least intimately, from the Aurelian Wall, then from the Colosseum, the Pantheon, the Forum, the Stadium, and then piece by piece, from the Vatican, the Diocletian, the Capitoline galleries of sculpture, is a very positive soul,

all of one piece, so to speak, in which it is useless
to search for delicate shades, the mystery of suggestion, a meaning other than the meaning which, in a
profound enough sense, is on the surface. All these
walls, columns, triumphal arches, the façade of the
Pantheon, have nothing to tell us beyond what they
were meant to tell; and they were meant to answer
certain very definite purposes, and to do their work
splendidly indeed, but without caprice. This simplicity of purpose is what makes Roman architecture
so much more satisfying than even fine Renaissance
architecture; and there is little fine Renaissance
work in Rome: the Cancellaria, a palace or two.
In architecture, more perhaps than in any other
art, nothing is so easily comprehended, so immediate
in its appeal to the instinct, as that greatest art,
which is classic. Think for a moment of St Peter's,
while you stand before the outer wall of the
Colosseum. That shell of rough stone-work, from
which every trace of ornamentation is gone, gives,
even at first sight, a sense of satisfaction, because
of the easy way in which those perfectly natural
proportions answer to the unconscious logic of the
eye, notwithstanding the immensity of the scale on
which they are carried out; while St Peter's leaves
you bedazed, wondering, inquiring, as before a pro-
blem of which you have not the key. For beauty
of detail, for the charm which is not the mathematical
charm of proportion, the moral charm of strength,
the material charm of grandeur, do not come to

Rome. You will find no detail neglected, for all detail is part of a whole; but you will find no detail over which the workman has grown amorous, into which he has put something of his soul, over and above the work of his hands.

To the Roman mind, as I have come to realise it for myself, after a winter in Rome spent in trying to make my general notion of these things particular, the world about one was always a very real, very desirable thing, quite enough for one's whole needs in a life which was at once a brief flutter of that winged thing, "animula, vagula, blandula," and also a moment which it was possible to perpetuate, by the work of one's hands, or the hands of slaves, working to order. In a world which seemed to lie at their feet, conquered, the sense of power, which the Romans had in so actual a degree, sharpened their desire to appropriate all the resources of what lay there before them, to enjoy its whole beauty, and to leave behind them, by their own effort, the assurance of what they had so vividly enjoyed. That monument of the baker, outside the Porta Maggiore, made to imitate the homely utensils of his trade, and still telling us that Marcus Vergilius Erysaces, who lies under those stones, sold his bread in the city, seems to me a significant indication of this resolute hold on the earth, on the day's work, and this resolution to perpetuate it. It is the more significant, because for the most part a mere citizen in Rome must have counted for very little.

As the world was for Rome, so Rome was for the State, and the State, after all, was for the Cæsars.

And so it is that we find the one really satisfying work in sculpture left by the Romans to be the Antinous, repeated over and over again, in an almost mechanical carrying out of the will of Hadrian, but coming, at its best, to a kind of perfection. Antinous is the smile of the eternity of youth, and the smile is a little sad, for all its gracious acceptance of the sunlight. It is sad with youth's sensitive consciousness of the first cold breath of wind which comes to trouble that sunlight; a wistfulness which is the wistfulness of animals, and in which the soul and its regrets have no part. Perfect bodily sensitiveness; the joy and sadness which are implicit in mere human breathing; a simplicity of sensation which comes at once into the delightful kingdom of things, which we are so painful in our search for, and thus attains a sort of complexity, or its equivalent, without knowing it; life taken on its own terms, and without preference of moment to moment: it is all this that I find in the grave, and smiling, and unthinking, and pensive head of Antinous, in that day-dream of youth, just conscious enough of its own felicity for so much the more heightened an enjoyment of that passing moment.

II

Looking at Antinous, or at a young Roman model who lies on those spectacular steps of the Trinità de' Monti to-day, you realise that the Romans were born without a soul, and that in all these centuries of Christendom they have never acquired one. It has been the genius of the Catholic religion, whose temporal seat, so appropriately, has always been at Rome, to divine and to respond to this temperamental tendency of the people who have given it power. At Rome it is natural to found empires; the seven hills await them. Religion never could be mystical at Rome; it must have its part in the world, with all the power of the world, and all the world's hold on temporal felicity, and it is by an appeal to after all largely the Pagan sentiment in life and thought that the Popes have been able to succeed the Cæsars. Never was any "mystical city of God" so solidly based on the stable powers of the earth. Church has succeeded temple, and you find the church superincumbent, quite literally, as in San Clemente, stratum above stratum, the chapel of Mithra under the apse of the Christian basilica; or, as in San Lorenzo fuori le Mura, where church after church, built over and into one another, is supported by columns, crowded with friezes, set together without design or order, out of ancient temples or palaces. Just as the theatre, dancing, music, were a part or appendage of the State religion, so the Church has taken to itself all that is finest in spectacle, all that is rarest in singing. Those perfumed and golden gifts of the three old Magi to the young Christ, the gift of the world and its delicacies, were not given in vain. All the churches in Rome are full of incense and gold.

To see St Peter's is to realise all that is strongest, most Roman, nothing that is subtle or spiritual, in the power of the Church. This vast building, the largest church in the world, imposes itself upon you, where-ever you are in Rome; you see the dome from the Alban or the Sabine hills, from which the whole city seems dwindled to a white shadow upon a green plain. Before it lies all Rome, behind it the vague desolation of fruitless fields, ruinous houses, a mouldering wall, a few ragged trees. I climbed one evening, about sunset, on a day when the sky itself had the desolation of brooding storms, to the strip of narrow, untrodden ground behind it, which rises from the Via Scaccia, going down on the other side to the Via della Zecca. It stood there hiding the whole city and half the sky, a vast grey bulk; now and again the moon, looking through a rift in the clouds, touched the leaden roof with a finger of light; the cypresses, seeming to lean against the white walls at the base, turned blacker, a few gas lamps shone about it like gold candles about the high altar; and gradually, as I watched, light after light sprang up out of the deep streets and precipitous houses, the hills grew darker and more vague, and the solid mass itself, now a looming greyness, seemed to float like a great shadow into the depths of the night. And always, by day, looked at from within or without, it is by its immensity, its spectacular qualities, that it is impressive. To walk across the floor is like taking a journey; voices chanting in a side chapel can only just be heard from the opposite aisle; and, looking at the four piers which support the dome, one remembers that the church of San Carlino alle Quattro Fontane, by no means a small church, is exactly the size of one of those four piers. Everything, the whole decoration, in order that it may be in proportion to the scale of the building, is exaggerated, and almost no detail bears an intimate examination, or can give one a separate sensation of pleasure; for the few lovely things, like Michelangelo's Pietà, are lost in little chapels, where they exist quietly, in their corners, like a fine, silent criticism of all this display, these florid Popes and angels, this noisy architectural rhetoric. And St Peter's, impressing you, as it certainly does, with its tremendous size, strength, wealth, and the tireless, enduring power which has called it into being, holds you at a distance, with the true ecclesiastical frigidity. You learn here how to distinguish between what is emotional and what is properly ecclesiastical in the Catholic Church. St Peter's is entirely positive, dogmatic, the assertion of the supremacy of the Church over the world; never mystic, as in one of those dim Spanish cathedrals, that of Barcelona, for instance; nor yet fantastic, full of strange, precious wonders of the world, brought from far off, as in St Mark's. It is florid, spectacular, but never profane; suggesting, as it does, what is the strength, and what are also the metaphysical limitations of the Church, it never suggests, as St Mark's does, the human curiosities which may become a strange vice, as easily as a singular virtue. Nor is it, like St Mark's, in the midst of the city, where the heart of the city beats, where one sees a homely crowd wandering in and out all day long, looking in on the way home from market, as one might look in for a moment at a friend's house.

High Mass at St Peter's, as I saw it on Christmas Day, said by Cardinal Rampolla, was an impressive ceremony, indeed, but it was said mainly to a crowd of curious strangers. The large, rigid figure in the red robes and the gold mitre, who sat there under his golden vestments, lifting a white gloved hand on whose third finger shone the emerald ring set with diamonds, performed the sacred functions with a dignity which was a little weary, and in the priest's expressionless way, with that air of fixed meditation (as of a continual commerce with heaven) which is the Church's manner of expressing disapproval of the world. Where I seemed to see a real devotion was in the peasants from the Campagna, who passed

with their rough cloaks rolled round them, and
kissed St Peter's foot devoutly, leaning their foreheads against it; the women carefully rubbing the
toe with their handkerchiefs before kissing it. I
saw the same deep feeling in a fifteenth-century
church into which I went that afternoon, S. Agostino,
a church famed for its devotion. A whole wall was
covered with little gilt-framed votive offerings, silver
hearts, and pious vows, and in front of them many
poor old women sat and knelt, praying with closed
eyes; others lifted their children to kiss the foot
of Sansovino's patrician Virgin, the compassionate
Madonna del Parto. I found a different, but perhaps not less sincere company of worshippers, in
San Luigi dei Francesi, before that screen of candles,
like burning gold, gold light rising flamelike out of
gilt candlesticks, which enshrined for their devotion
the unseen presence of the Sacrament. But at the
midnight Mass in the same church, which was
attended by a special permission, I was once more
in that atmosphere of positive, unspiritual things
which I had breathed in St Peter's, and which
seemed to me so typical of Rome. The church
was filled to its farthest corner by a brilliant
crowd; the music, played by organ, harp, and
strings, and sung by somewhat uncertain voices,
was florid and brilliant; and far off, at the golden
end of the church, white against the gold light,
seven rows of candles rising like an arch of pure
gold, the priests moved through the sacred ritual.

Near me were some Italians, two of them women of the finest aristocratic type, with faces carved like cameos, a touch of cruelty in their dark, vivid, reticent dignity; and these faces, looking on as at a show, and prepared to look away the moment it was no longer amusing, seemed to bring all the strength of the world's hold on one into the perfumed atmosphere of the place. Looking, as I could not but look, at these beautiful Pagan faces, perfect as Roman medals, I felt that they were Rome, and that Rome was at least sure of this world, whatever her admiration, her curiosity, her possible dreams, of another.

III

"The grandeur that was Rome": that phrase of Poe's sums up perfectly the impression which Rome, even now, makes upon the observer. The secret of what is most impressive there is the choice (miraculous, we are led to suppose, and can well believe) of its site. A city built upon seven hills, hills which have arranged themselves, naturally, with such an art of impressive composition, can have no rival among the cities of the world in its appeal to the sense of material grandeur. That the Senate should throne itself upon the Capitol, that the palaces of the Cæsars should have been on the Palatine or the Esquiline, was an almost incalculable

aid to the pomp of State. St Peter's, seen in the
sky from all Rome, thrones Catholicism on a similar
eminence. Everything in Rome impresses by its
height, by an amplitude of adjusted proportions,
which is far more than the mere equivalent of vast
spaces covered, as in London, invisible for its very
size. The pride of looking down, the pride of
having something to look up to, are alike satisfied
for the Romans, by what nature and art have done
for Rome.

This Roman grandeur began by being colossally
simple. I find all the grandeur of Rome in
even so late a work as the Aurelian Wall, and
that is nothing but a bare, brown, precipitous line
of masonry, patched with the mendings of all the
ages. The Colosseum, the Pantheon, for all their
original splendour of decoration, still exist with such
potency, now that they are reduced to the bare
elements of their construction, because the simplicity
of that construction was the primary concern of
Vespasian and Titus, of Agrippa and Hadrian, in
building them. Effect is aimed at, and the effect
is always that of impressing by size ; but the effect
is sought legitimately, with the finest materials,
their most natural, however sumptuous, arrangement,
and that Roman way of going straight to an end,
like their roads, though at the cost of an army of
men, a treasury of gold. In the work of the Middle
Ages, of the Renaissance, of the seventeenth century,
we find the same effect aimed at, but with a sumptu-

ousness not duly subordinated, and turning frequently (as in the extravagances of the typical Bernini) into colossal bad taste. Yet still, to this moment, Rome is the most pompous, the most magnificent, of Western cities. Was there ever a more imposing public square than that vast, florid Piazza del Popolo, by which, before the days of the railway, strangers entered Rome; almost nowhere entirely commendable in detail, but with what an art of effect in its remote corners, into which no crowd can stretch, its three long, straight, narrow vistas into the city, its terraced and columned heights, its great gateway? The square in which St Peter's stands, with that colonnade which Bernini set up in his one moment of genius; the dark, irregular, half-concealed palace of the Vatican holding on to a corner of the great church; the square itself, with its obelisk, the two fountains, the stones worn by all the pilgrims of the world; no other square makes quite the same appeal to one, or suggests so much of the world's history. And how impressive, certainly how sumptuous, are all these immense, never quite architecturally satisfying churches, heaped against the sky at the corner of every square, dignifying the poverty of even the humblest streets, leaving, like San Paolo fuori le Mura, infinite riches run to waste in the unpopulated Campagna! You can scarcely walk for five minutes in any direction without coming on something, perhaps incongruous where it is, like the eleven Corinthian columns of Hadrian's Temple of Neptune, forty feet high, now filled up with modern brickwork, and made into the Exchange; something absolutely startling, something vast and sudden, it may be only the Trevi Fountain, it may be the Theatre of Marcellus, the Capitol itself. And the appropriate *décor* of life awaits every occasion, ready set; for what occasion is there in life which was not anticipated and prepared for, with learned, foreseeing taste, centuries ago, in those times when Rome had perfected the arts of life as now only the Eastern races ever dream of perfecting them? Think, in the baths of Caracalla or of Diocletian, among the trees and ruins of the Palatine; or, with less of the historic effort, in the gardens of the Villa Albani, with their alleys of shaven box, carved into niches for statues; of the Villa Borghese, with their avenues of ilex, their grassy amphitheatre; of the Villa Doria-Pamphili, which is like an English park, laid out by a French gardener; in the Bosco of the Villa Medici, wild and delicate, with its staircase going up between the trees to the sky; think what a *décor* lies before one, gone to waste, or at least wasted, for a life of the most triumphant pleasure! To live in Rome is to understand all the coloured and spectacular vices of the Cæsars, all the elaborate sins of the Renaissance. Occasions so great as these have gone, but the possibilities remain, awaiting only their opportunity.

IV

Rome is a sea in which many worlds have gone down, and its very pavement is all in waves; so that to drive through these narrow streets, and across these broad squares, in which there is no footway over which a wheel may not drive, is like rocking in a boat on slightly uneasy water. The soil everywhere heaves over still buried ruins, which may hold (who knows?) another Apoxyomenos. And, as no other great city in the world is, the whole of Rome is one vast museum, in which the very galleries, palaces, churches, which contain the finest of its treasures, are themselves but single items in that museum which is Rome. And what gives to all this precisely its special charm, and also its special value to the student, is that Rome is still a living city, the capital of a nation, and with an actual life of its own, which, often enough, can be seen in its direct descent from antiquity. The Roman people have always had a sense of the continuity of their national life, of their literal part in the inheritance of their ancestors. One sees it, sometimes with a quaint grotesqueness, in the simple-minded way in which, just as they Christianised Pagan temples, so they have always taken to themselves and turned to their own uses the monuments of all the ages: Pasquino, Marforio, Madama Lucrezia, the Bocca della Verità; the religion of one age becoming the mouthpiece for the

B

satire or criticism of the next, as the Pagan gods in
exile, in the Christian Middle Ages, became demons,
haunting the souls of men with their perilous beauty.
One sees it, at the present day, in that singular
deification of Vittorio Emanuele, which is really an
apotheosis, after the manner of the apotheoses of
the Roman emperors ; and quite after their ruthless
manner is that waste of thousands of pounds in the
destruction of certain old streets, which were beautiful, for the proper view of an equestrian statue,
which will be hideous.   And then, in the actual
museums, the palace of the Vatican, the palace of
the Conservatori, the baths of Diocletian, what a
prepared atmosphere one finds, and how much more
at home in these courts, frescoed halls, papal
summer-houses, Carthusian cloisters, is all this white,
chosen humanity of statues, which, if they "remember their august abodes," must certainly pine less for
Greece, which they left so early, than any other
marble beings in the world.   Since I have been in
Rome I have realised, for myself, many things about
Greek art, which not all the study of sculpture in
London, Paris, and Berlin had taught me ; and I
have been able to see it, not only as the greatest,
the most " classic " art of the world, but as the most
living, responsive, intimately delightful.   And this is
certainly because I have seen it where it could be
seen more like something in its natural place, less
like something on show, than anywhere out of
Greece.

And in painting, too, one has the opportunity of making certain not unsimilar discoveries. Rome is not rich in easel-pictures, nor yet in altar-pieces, but it is only in Rome that it is possible to realise, to the full extent of their gifts and limitations, the pictorial genius of Michelangelo, of Raphael, and of Pinturicchio. Michelangelo in the decoration of the Sistine Chapel, Raphael in the decoration of the Stanze and Logge, Pinturicchio in the decoration of the Appartamento Borgia, of the Vatican, is seen working as the painter loves to work, in the one really satisfying way in which he can work, architecturally, for the adornment of a given space, which is part of the essential life of a building. And so these frescoes, as no picture in a museum could ever be, are an actual part of Rome, precisely as much a part of it as the Vatican itself.

In the Sistine Chapel there are admirable paintings by Botticelli, by Signorelli, by Perugino, but one can see nothing there but Michelangelo. And the emotion of first seeing this immense world created by Michelangelo seized me with a delighted awe, such as I could imagine to have stirred in the soul of Adam when he awoke and beheld the world. Other things are beautiful, exquisite, subtle, but these seem to contain all beautiful and exquisite and subtle things, and to disregard them. In the passion of this overwhelming life which burns through every line, there is for once the creating joy of the artist, flawless, unimpaired, unchecked, fulfilling its desire as not even the Greeks have done; for desire, in them, was restrained by a sense of delicate harmony, to which it was the triumphant self-sacrifice of their art to conform. Here we have no sense of even so much of mortal concession to the demands of immortality; but the unbounded spirit seems to revel in the absoluteness of its freedom. Here, at last, here indeed for the first time, is all that can be meant by sublimity; a sublimity which attains its pre-eminence through no sacrifice of other qualities; a sublimity which (let us say it frankly) is amusing. I find the magnificent and extreme life of these figures as touching, intimate, and direct in its appeal, as the most vivid and gracious realism of any easel-picture; God, the Father and the Son, the Virgin, the men and women of the Old Testament, the Sibyls, the risen dead of the Last Judgment, all these tremendous symbols of whatever has been divined by the spirit or sought out by the wisdom of the ages, crowd upon one with the palpable, irresistible nearness of the people who throng one in one's passage through the actual world. It seemed to me then, it still seems to me, strange that I should have felt it, but never before had I felt so much at home among paintings, so little of a mere spectator. One seems to be of the same vivid and eternal world as these joyous and meditative beings, joyous and meditative even in hell, where the rapture of their torment broods in eyes and limbs with the same energy as the rapture

of God in creation, of the woman in disobedience, or
of Isaiah in vision. They are close to one, I think,
partly because they are so far away; because no
subtlety in the eyes or lips, no delicacy in the fold
of garments, none of the curious and discoverable
ways by which art imitates and beautifies nature,
can distract one from the immediate impress of such
passionate and obsessing life. Art ceases to approach
one indirectly, through this sense or that, through
colour, or suggested motion, or some fancied outlook
of the soul; it comes straight to one, boldly, seizing
one at once by that instinct of immediate recognition,
by which, except here, only perhaps the direct works
of God have ever approached and revealed themselves
to the soul of man.

Now turn to Raphael. Here, on the contrary,
we have art so obvious in its concealment of art
that it becomes the idol of the crowd, and ceases
to interest the more curious dreamer before pictures.
Raphael is the instinctively triumphant perfection of
the ideal of the average man; he is what scarcely
the greatest of painters can be, and what only
mediocre painters have desired to be. Here is the
simplicity of what is called inspiration: the ease of
doing, better than any one else, what the greater
number would like, better than anything else, to do.
And he is miraculous; yet a miracle which just fails
to interest one; because, I think, he is essentially
exterior, and his pictures a dream of the hand,
rather than a dream of the soul. Even that

peace which he can convey with so delicate a
power, seems to me rather the slumber than the
ecstasy of peace. His Madonnas have no foresight
in their eyes of the seven swords with which the
divine child is to pierce their breasts. His gracious
saints have never, before they attained sanctity,
suffered all the enlightening ardours of sin. His
martyrs have no memory, either of death, by which
they have passed, or of heaven, to which they have
come. All the persons of his pictures live, somewhat unthinkingly, in the moment which their
gesture perpetuates; they have but that gesture.
We see eternity in the moment of fierce meditation
which Michelangelo calls up before us, as if
thought in the brows and hands were about to
relax or resolve itself into some other of the unaccountable moods of so elemental a being. In the
painful, intense face of a Velasquez we see the
passionate frailties, the morbid, minute hatreds of a
long race of just such suffering and reticent beings.
And in the smile which wanders, lurking in the
imperceptible corner of lip or eyelid, across the
faces of Leonardo, we see the enigma of whatever
is most secret, alluring, inexplicable, in the mysterious
charm of human beauty; that look which seems to
remember, and is perhaps only a forgetfulness.
But the people of Raphael live in the content of
that one gracious moment in which they lift their
hands in prayer or benediction, or open their un-
troubled eyes to that moment's sunlight.

The art of Pinturicchio, which can now, since the
opening of the Appartamento Borgia in the Vatican,
be studied more completely at Rome than even at
Siena, is another, a more primitive, but not less
individual art. Those frescoes, simply as decorations, are as beautiful as any decorations that were
ever done; and they are at once an arabesque, in
which everything seems to exist simply in order
that it may be a moment's beautiful colour on a
wall, and a piece of homely realism, in which every
figure seems to be a portrait, and every animal, tree,
and jewel to be painted for its own sake. There
is not a little naïveté in the design, a technique
in which there is none of the confident sureness
of hand of either Raphael or Michelangelo, but a
certain hesitation, an almost timid recourse to such
expedients as the use of stucco in relief, and even
of painted wood, glued upon the flat surface to
represent a tower or a gateway. But you feel
that the man has something to say, that, to be
more accurate, he sees pictures; and that this
simple and sumptuous and real and imaginary
world, which he has called into being in order that
it may remind us of the world about us, and be
more beautiful, and so be a delight to the eyes
and a repose to the soul, is not only an unsurpassed
piece of decoration, but the revelation of a temperament to which beauty was perhaps more beautiful
for its own sake than to any other painter. Pinturicchio loves the world, animals, trees, human

faces, the elegance of men and women in courtly,
coloured dresses, youth with its simple pride of
existence, kings for their gold and purple robes,
saints for the divine calm of their eyelids and the
plaintive grace of their slim hands, all the world's
beauty as it comes up like the flower of the grass,
and especially that beauty which takes no thought
of itself; and he loves it with so simple and humble
and absorbing a love that he paints it just as he
sees it, almost without thinking of his own share in
the work. That is why this select and coloured
world of his, in which there is no passionate or
visionary life, as in Michelangelo, nor that composed and conscious presence in time and space of
the people of Raphael, lives with such simplicity, as
if filled with a calm and joyous sense of its own
beauty. To live under the decorations of Michelangelo would be as exhausting as to live in a
world in which every person was a person of
genius. To live amongst the decorations of
Raphael would be to live amongst people of too
placid, too amiable disposition, and too limited
intelligence; it would become a weariness. But
one need never cease to live happily amongst the
men and women whom Pinturicchio saw walking
in beautiful robes, that were never woven so finely
by hands, in meadows of gold flowers, that never
grew out of the brown earth, always finding
heaven, a heaven of chrysoprase and chalcedony,
at a turn of the way, and without surprise; for

these and their abode have the beauty that we desire to find in the world, in what is most homely, obvious, and frequent in it, the beauty that is there, if we could see it, and the beauty that for the most part we do not see, because we are too sophisticated, too conscious of ourselves, and because we discover too thoughtful a consciousness of themselves in natural things.

V

To realise the greatness of Rome, it is not enough to have seen the Colosseum, St Peter's, the churches, palaces, ruins, squares, fountains, and gardens; you may have seen all these, and yet not have seen the most beautiful possession of Rome: the Campagna. Seen from the Alban hills, Rome is a mere cluster of white houses in a desert, a desert as variable in colour as the sky. Lost in that wilderness, a speck between that wilderness and the sky, it seems a mere accident in a visible infinity. And now remember that this vast Campagna is simply the pleasure park of Rome; that it is left there, feverous and unproductive, the loveliest of ruins, in order that Rome may have the pride of possessing it; and think if any city in the world possesses so costly and magnificent a luxury.

It is one of the many delicate surprises of Rome to come suddenly, at the end of a street which had seemed lost in the entanglements of the city, upon a glimpse of the Campagna or the hills. And those hills, rising up from the plain to the sky, their soft lines, under certain weather, indistinguishable from either, opalescent, changing colour as the wind scatters or heaps the clouds, as sunlight or scirocco passes over them, have something of the untiring charm, the infinite variety, of the sea. Drive a little way into the Campagna, and you might be on the Pampas, or in the desert which is about the ruins of Thebes. An almost audible silence descends upon you, in which the world seems asleep. A shepherd leans motionless upon his staff; the sheep move drowsily about him; and you hear the tinkle of the bell.

To see Tivoli, loud and white with waterfalls, a little grey town set upon grey and cloven rocks, fringed with the silvery green of olive trees; to see any one of the *castelli*, one would willingly cross a whole country; and they lie, Frascati, Albano, Genzano, Marino, Ariccia, Rocca di Papa, at the very gates of Rome, within the compass of one day's drive. These *castelli* are all fantastic and improbable; white, huddled, perched like flights of white birds that have settled there; hanging over volcanic chasms that have burst into lakes, fertilised into vines and olives; wild trees, their grey trunks leaning this way and that, seeming to race up and down the hillside, like armies meeting in battle; each *castello* with its own rococo villas, like incrustations upon the rock; each *castello* set on its own hill, as if it had drawn up the ladder after having climbed there : a little city of refuge from the perils of the plain. They hold the Alban Lake between them, and Lake Nemi, which sleeps with the deepest sleep of any lake I have ever seen, in the most restful arms of land. And each has its own aspect. Frascati, as one turns in and out of its streets, opening suddenly on vague glimpses, as if cut by the sides of a frame, is like a seaside village ; and one cannot help imagining the wash of waves, instead of the grassy plain of the Campagna, at the end of those coiling streets. Rocca di Papa is like an eagle's nest, perched high on the mountain, with its shady square in front of the little church where you hear old women praying aloud. Marino has an air of the country, with its fierce men, its somewhat bold, handsome women, its thronging children. Ariccia hangs picturesquely against the very side of the hill, jutting out into space. Each has its variety of primitive life, of rococo architecture, of running water, of trees, of volcanic rock, of lake scenery. And for those who care greatly for the delicate shading of colours as they change over a sensitive landscape, to look from these heights is to look down, from dawn till sunset, upon a paradise of the daintiest colours in the world, in that jewelled desert which lies about Rome.

But the Campagna is most wonderful, most itself, at sunset ; and sunset in Rome should be seen from the Via Appia, as I saw it during a memorable drive in mid-winter. Looking back from the mound beyond the Casal Rotondo, Rome seemed far off, dwindled by

distance, all its towers and domes and roofs white,
set in the hollow of the hills. Nearer to me, Frascati,
a white sparkle upon the dark Alban hills; between,
along the sky, the Apennines, their snow lying
caressingly against the clouds; and below, all around
me, the desert of the Campagna, the long grey line of
the aqueducts seeming to impress itself, with a certain
insistency, upon the otherwise timeless waste of the
great plain. A church bell sounded faintly, like the
sound of a cow-bell, from a little white church on the
Via Appia Nuova; the air was still, clear, cold, with
a marvellous serenity in its soft brightness; and as I
looked across the Campagna, going out desolately
towards the sea, I could just distinguish a light
shining along the line of dark trees at the edge of
the horizon. Hearing a slow creaking of wheels, I
looked down, and saw in a road two lounging oxen
drawing a load of silvery ilex boughs. Two peasants
went by, lounging like the oxen, in their long-haired
garments of undressed skins; shepherds who had
come down from the Apennines for the winter, with
their flocks and herds, and had encamped upon the
plain, in the little conical huts which rise out of it
so strangely. Sunset was beginning, and, as we
drove back along the Via Appia, the clouds which
had obscured the sun cleared away, and the sky
seemed to be washed with colours which were at
once fiery and watery; greens of an inexpressibly
luminous delicacy, paler and softer than any grass
or leaf that ever grew, but with the ardour in them

of growing things; pinks that were like the inner
petals of rose-leaves, flushing on the horizon to a
fierce golden red, which burned in the tops of the
trees like a conflagration, and at the edges floating
away into paler and paler gold, and from that into
the green of moonlit water, and from that into a blue
which was the colour of shallow water, under very
faint sunlight, a blue which deepened overhead into
the vast outstretched dome of the sky. The air
grew chill, with that intense cold which seems to
come down out of the sky upon Rome for an hour
after sunset. We drove back, along the straight
road, between the ruined tombs which had once
stood at the gates of the villas of Romans, and
which stand now, in their ruins, seeming to look, as the
Romans loved to look, on the road which was the
world's highway; that long road leading into the
Eternal City (upon which, indeed, the ends of the
earth are still visibly come) out of the vague world.
In so beautiful a desolation, at which the soul shivers
away into that loneliness which is the soul's ecstasy
before eternal things, I said to myself that here, if anywhere upon earth, God and man had worked together
to show at one glimpse all the glory of the world.

VI

Perhaps my most agreeable recollection of a
winter spent in Rome is the recollection of in-

numerable drives with a friend in the Roman Campagna and about the Castelli Romani. The Comte
de B., after a lifetime of disinterested travelling,
in which he has trained his eyes to a perfect sus-
ceptibility, and his judgment to a perfect impartiality,
in the noting and comparison of so much of the
world's scenery, has come finally to a deliberate
preference of this scenery about Rome as the most
beautiful in the world, a deliberate choice of it as
the scenery most appropriate, at all events, to the
demands of his own temperament, the requirements
of his own meditations. And it is through his
eyes, certainly, that I first learned to see the Campagna, which, like all profound beauty, does not
reveal itself to all, with the insolent challenge of
Alps, the feminine seductiveness of meadow-lands;
and I cannot evoke for myself the spectacle of the
Roman landscape without seeing in its midst so
difficult, so constant, so learned a lover of it; for
this strange, attractive figure, the traveller, the
student of race, the student of history, with his
courtly violence, his resolute pieties, his humorous
prejudices softening the rigour of a singular spiritual
equanimity, his reticent, self-absorbed, and yet
gracious and affectionate temperament, has come to
seem to me himself an inevitable figure in that
landscape.

The beauty of the Campagna is a soft, gradual,
changing beauty, whose extreme delicacy is made
out of the action upon one another of savage and

poisonous forces. The line of the Alban mountains, against the clear sky, is the most harmonious line of mountains that I have ever seen; but its pathetic grace, in which there is almost the appeal of music, comes to it from the tumultuous caprice of volcanic fires. The great plain, which, seen from the hills, is like a gently undulating sea, covered with soft and variable tints as the sunlight wanders across it, is a desert of lava, barren soil, and lank herbage, discoloured grass and the far from "tufted" asphodel. The malaria which always lurks there has thinned and withered and bent the few shepherds and herdsmen who are its only inhabitants. Its silence is the silence of desolation. It is ridged with broken aqueducts, strewn with the fragments of the tombs and villas of Romans. Before Rome was, it was Latium, the birthplace of the Latin people. It hides under it the Catacombs of the Christians. All the changes of the earth and of the world have passed over it, ruining it with elaborate cruelty; and they have only added subtlety to its natural beauty, and memories to that beauty of association which is a part of the spirit of places.

But the charm of the Campagna depends also, more than most landscapes, on weather, on the hour at which one sees it; and it has different aspects, seems to reveal to one a different secret, as one approaches it from this gate or that. Our drive was usually timed to end with sunset, and sunset is the most surprising and illusive hour at which to see the Campagna. I remember the first sunset I ever saw there. We had driven around the deserted outer side of the Aurelian Wall, between the *canne*, rustling loudly, rattling against one another, in the rising *tramontana*, and the tall brown wall, in which the stones are of every age and recall every ruler of Rome. The air was cold and bright, and as we came near the Porta San Paolo, sunset was beginning to streak a pale sky with faint bands of rose and green, against which I saw the cypresses of Shelley's graveyard and the Pyramid of Cestius. The sky flushed, moment by moment, with brighter and brighter, yet always delicate, colour, a faint rose which reddened to fire, splashing with sidelong jets of flame the pallid green which brightened miraculously to a watery colour as green as grass, yet as luminous as moonlight. Green melted into gold, red into the faintest of rose, as if an inner heat burned them, and every colour was reflected in diminishing shades, above and below, upon the sky itself. And this light in the sky seemed to reflect itself, as in a mirror, all over the Campagna, which changed sensitively as every colour changed in the sky. In a time of scirocco, when I have seen the vapour rolling in from the hills, the whole plain has seemed to wither into an ashen greyness; at noon, under steady sunlight, it has shimmered with gold; at night, when I have climbed a high wooded bank which lies outside the Porta del Popolo, I have seen it lying under its network of silver mist, the Tiber hurrying through it, curved like a crescent. And always, closing in the plain as with a magic circle, there has been the soft line of the Alban hills, the sharper indentations of the Sabine hills, and beyond, the snow upon the Apennines.

The beauty of the little hill-towns which rise out of the Campagna, like rocks rising out of the sea, has really the character of a kind of inland sea-coast, in which the houses themselves take a precipitous and rocky air, clinging, as they do at Ariccia, to a scant foothold over a gulf, or, at Rocca di Papa, to the bare side of the mountain; and they have, along with this shy and withdrawn savagery of aspect, to which the quite recent legends of brigandage add a certain confirmation, something almost artificial in their exquisite poise, their spectacular appropriateness of detail, the happy accidents of their grouping, and the rococo adornment of their villas, built for Popes and princes. It is by their artificiality that they seem to attach themselves to Rome, by that side of them which is delicate and ornate; their ruggedness, the freshness of their mountain air, the colour in the rough cheeks of their peasants, the flavour of their wine and flowers, are all their own, and have nothing in common with anything Roman. Only Tivoli seems to me in a sense Roman, one of the great things of Rome, on the same natural scale as the great buildings there; what is artificial in

c

its waterfalls and gorges and the terraced Villa
d'Este being done consummately, and with a complete harmony of adaptation.

And, like the Campagna, these *castelli* have their
secrets, which are not quite ready to reveal themselves to every comer. At Frascati, for instance,
even the Villa Aldobrandini is, in a sense, one of
the show-villas; that villa which, if you read closely
enough in Pater's "Marius," you will find described
as the house of a certain "aristocratic poet who
loved every sort of superiorities," where Marius
meets Apuleius. "Whereupon," we are told, "the
numerous cascades of the precipitous garden of the
villa, framed in the doorway of the hall, fell into a
harmless picture, in its place among the pictures
within, and hardly more real than they." Yes, even
there I do not find the intimacy, the penetrating
strangeness, of the neglected gardens of the Villa
Falconieri, higher up on the other side of the climbing roadway, entered by a gate flowered through by
the whole body of an immense, twisted, very ancient
tree, which has been allowed so fantastic a whim
of growth. There is a little lake on a plateau at
the highest point of those gardens, which I shall
remember even if I forget Lake Nemi itself, and
that "mirror of Diana" is the most purely beautiful
lake I have ever seen. This space of dark water
is closed in on three sides by tall, motionless
cypresses, their solemn green, menacing enough in
itself, reflected like great cubes of blackness, point-

ing downwards at the sky. The waters are always dark, even in full sunlight; they have always that weight upon them of the funereal trees which stand between them and the sun; and through the cypresses you can see Rome, far away, beyond the gardens, the stacked vines, the olive-trees, and the indefinite wilderness, set there like a heap of white stones. I scarcely know what it is that this unaccountable scene awaits; but it seems to wait. Disillusioned lovers might walk there, chill even on a day of sun, seeing their past perhaps in that distant glimpse of Rome, their future in those cypress-shadowed depths, and their present in the narrow strip of brown earth between those two infinitudes.

Scenery so liberal as this scenery of the Roman Campagna lends itself, on their own terms, to many minds. By whatever side human things and the history of the world interest you, on that side chiefly will you feel the attraction of the Campagna. To the friend, in whose company I frequented it, it was a mirror of very definite thoughts, memories, speculations, with which the history and religion of Rome had to do. Here, he would remind me, at that bend of the Tiber, Cleopatra's barge passed, rowing hard for Egypt; there, at the cross-roads on the Via Appia, Christ appeared to St Peter, where the little church still asks the question, "Domine, quo vadis?" Here, on the Via Ostense, a small chapel marks the spot where St Peter and St Paul took leave of one another before each went to his martyrdom ; farther on, at the Tre Fontane, where the Trappists' friends, the birds, sing among avenues of eucalyptus, St Paul was beheaded. To my friend every stone had its precise memory, its legend or record. And that, certainly, is the most fruitful way of seeing the Campagna, though, indeed, one ignorant or heedless of these things might still come to prefer this to all other scenery, for its own sake, for its mere natural sensitiveness to one's moods and the sunlight.

VII

We love cities for their gracious weather, as we love persons for their amiable dispositions ; and Rome, even in winter, shows frequently a marvellous equanimity of temper. I have had, in December and January, weeks of uninterrupted sunshine, in which every day's promenade ended naturally, as it should, with sunset. And that perilous shiver of cold which comes over city and Campagna in the hour after sunset gives just that astringent touch which is needed for the completion of all merely pleasant beauty. But happiness in Rome, certainly, comes and goes with the wind and the sunshine. Withdraw the sun, and Rome is like a face from which the smile has faded ; change the wind, and one's own disposition changes with it. Driving one day in the Campagna, outside the Porta Furba, I

saw the scirocco. The hills above Frascati were a
little dimmed with clouds ; gradually a vast, white,
rolling mist came violently up out of the sky beyond
the hills; soft, stealthy, pendulous, undulating, irresistible, it came coiling rapidly onward, as if a poisonous life had taken shape and came serpentlike upon
Rome. Under a chill rain these narrow streets,
with their wrinkled stones in which the rain gathers,
become desolate in an instant; and indoors, in these
houses without fires, without chimneys, life becomes
intolerable. Living, as one is apt to do here, on
one's sensations, how can any happiness be possible
in the absence of just what makes the happiness of
the sensations : gracious weather, the mere liberty
to feel without discomfort? By one's fireside in
London a storm of winter rain matters little enough.
But what does everything else in the world matter
here in a downpour of rain in winter?

And these people, one feels, are made for happiness, for the easy acceptance of things as they come.
There is a terrible poverty in Rome, of which the
beggars who await you at every street corner are
but too genuine a sign. The first gesture learnt by
the children of poor people in Rome is to hold
out their hands for alms ; they begin when they are
so young that they can only totter, and they are
still holding out their hands for alms when they can
only totter because they are so old. Yet another
sign of it I find in the 3000 cabmen of Rome, sitting
hungrily on their boxes, in their worm-eaten fur

coats, too lazy to do anything but sit there holding out their whips to solicit every passer, and unable to make a decent living even in a place so frequented by strangers and a place where every one drives. But even here, in these beggars and cabmen, is there not a certain participation, at all events, in that open-air life which is the felicity of Rome? " Abbiamo pazienza," say the poor people, and sit in the sun.

To poor and rich alike, the whole of every part of the open air of Rome is a personal property. People stand in the streets as if in their own drawing-rooms; and in the Corso, especially at that hour of the .afternoon when the thickest flow of carriages has passed, they stretch from side to side, forming into groups outside the Caffè Aragno and on both sides of the Piazza Colonna. But, if they can, they drive : Italians hate walking. This gives them a respect for anything on wheels, so that Rome is represented by its carriages, as Venice is repre-sented by its gondolas. They have even saintly warrant for it; for San Filippo Neri, one of their patron saints, and himself a typical Roman, set it down among his instructions to the faithful that, as a concession to the weakness of the flesh, it was permitted to keep a carriage. And the Romans have taken him so precisely at his word that they will live on macaroni and five soldi's worth of wine in order to keep a *carrozza*. Cardinals, again, are not allowed to walk in the streets ; they must drive in a closed carriage. So it is that Rome, more than any other city in which driving is a luxury rather than a necessity, is the city where one drives. The constant passing of carriages, in streets where two can scarcely pass abreast and where there is no footpath, procures one, indeed, one of the few disagreeable sensations of Rome : the sensation, whenever one walks, of a wheel about to descend on one's heel.

In the long, narrow, thronged Corso the press of carriages, as they go to and return from the Pincio, is so great that walking becomes difficult. But, all the same, I find that conventional drive along the Corso, through the Piazza del Popolo, up the winding terraces of the Pincio, the equivalent (and how much more than the equivalent !) of Hyde Park or the Bois de Boulogne, one of the most tolerable of all conventional drives. What I find specially charming is its universality, its equality. You will see the queen in her carriage with the red livery ; the nobility, the rich bourgeois, the shopkeepers, all with their families ; nurse-maids, women without hats, young clerks and young princes, passing and repassing, side by side, all seeming to be entirely contented with themselves, the fine air, the music, the marvellous view over Rome, in which the colours begin to group towards sunset. On those picturesque heights, high over the city; under those evergreen oaks by which the Romans delude themselves into thinking it is never winter; in sight of St Peter's in the sky, and all Rome, its roofs and domes, below;

without thought, but idly satisfied with the sunlight, with the band that plays to them their positive, un-shaded, soulless Italian music, Verdi or Mascagni, they pass and repass, proud of being Romans, even if they do not take the trouble to so much as glance at the daily miracle of Rome.

VIII

The carnival, which this year, for perhaps the first time in ten years, was really a carnival, is simply the personification of Roman idleness, and a gaiety which is a sort of tradition. I begin to see now the mean-ing of those idle people, dinnerless, and with shining boots and many rings, who stand in the Corso in front of the Caffè Aragno. To wear coloured dresses, to put on masks, to run in the streets all day and to dance all night, to chatter irresponsibly, to throw jokes and confetti about the air, and to forget that one is poor, that life has its to-morrow and has had its yesterday: this is happiness to the Romans, and their abandonment to it is contagious. It is very long since anything has given me so inspiriting and reckless a sense of the joy of life as the sight of these ardent smiling faces, in which mirth is never vulgar, but as natural as speech; and I find the mask, making all men humorously akin, the only form in which the idea of democracy is not intolerable. What a coloured whirl, in which all

Rome seemed to become a kaleidoscope! Everywhere a flight of white frilled things, Pierrots, Pulcinellas, darting, alighting, along a flowery way, like white birds; flowers by day and lights by night; the cars, the *moccoletti*; with, at night, the pathos of streets strewn with flowers and confetti, the smell of trodden flowers, the feast ended. On the afternoon of Mercoledì Grasso I began to make my way along the Corso at three, and I did not reach the Piazza del Popolo until half-past four. And that difficult way along the street, its windows all aflower with faces, a soft rain of coloured paper raindrops, the sharp hail of confetti falling all the way, flowers flying above one's head, settling on one's hat, tapping against one's cheek, was a lesson in the Italian temperament, its Southern capacity for simple enjoyment, for the true folly, that abandonment to the moment's whim in which there is none of the Northern brutality. Civilisation has sunk deeper into these people, in whom civility is a tradition; it has penetrated to the roots; and in this character, so positive, so unshaded, from which the energy has dwindled away, but not the simplicity, the charming and graceful naturalness, there is the same superficial, yet in its way sufficient, quality as in the fine finish of these faces, equally finished in the peasant and in the noble.

IX

Northern beauty, however fine may be the line of its contour, is never, for good or evil, a mere beauty of the body, a thing beginning with itself and ending in itself: it contains always a suggestion; it is haunted by a soul; it leaves for its completion something to the imagination. But in the beauty of Roman women there is no trace of spiritual beauty, none of the softness of charm; it is the calm, assured, unquestioning beauty of the flesh. These are faces which should be seen always in pure outline, for they are without melting curves, delicate and variable shades, or any of that suggestion which comes from anything but their own definite qualities, as they are in themselves. The faces of Roman women of the upper classes are cold, hard, finished and impenetrable as cameos. In a face which is at all beautiful you will not find a line which is not perfect, and this elegance and sureness of line goes with that complexion which is the finest of all complexions, pure ivory, and which carries with it the promise of a temperament in which there is all the subtlety of fire. The distinction between the properly aristocratic and the strictly plebeian face is, I think, less marked in Rome than in any city. Almost all Roman women have regular faces, the profile clearly cut and in a straight line; black hair, often with deep tones of blue in it, and sometimes curling crisply; dark eyes, often of a fine uniform brown, large, steady, profound, with that unmeaning profundity which means race, and which one sees in the Jewess, the gipsy. They have a truly Roman dignity, and beneath that the true fire, without which dignity is but the comely shroud of a corpse; and though there is not a trace in them of the soft, smiling, catlike air of the women of Venice, and not much of the vivid, hardy, uncaring provocativeness of the women of Naples, they are content to let you see in them that reasonable nearness to the animal which no Italian woman is ashamed to acknowledge. They have often a certain massiveness of build, which makes a child look like a young woman, and a young woman like a matron; but, for Italians, they are tall, and though one sees none of the trim Neapolitan waists, it is but rarely that one sees, even among the market-women bringing in their baskets on their heads, those square and lumpish figures which roll so comfortably through Venice.

The day on which to see the Roman populace most easily, most significantly, is the day of San Stefano, at that popular saint's church on the Cælian. The circular walls are covered with fifteenth-century paintings of martyrdoms, naïve saints, bold in colour and distressing in attitude, suffering all the tortures of pagan ingenuity. From early morning till late in the afternoon an incessant stream of people, mostly young people, out of all the alleys of Rome and from all the hills of the

Campagna, surges in and out of the narrow doorway,
where one is almost carried off one's feet in the
difficult passage.   Outside, where there are lines of
booths covered with sweets and toys, fruits and
cakes, the lane has the aspect of a fair.   Inside,
there is a service going on in the choir, but few pay
much heed to it; they have come to see the show,
and they make the round of all the martyrdoms.
The women, almost all bareheaded, stop at the door,
in the very press of the crowd, to pull out the folded
handkerchief and throw it over their heads, catching
the ends between their teeth.   And face after face,
as I watched them pass me, was absolutely beautiful;
now a Raphael Madonna, now a Roman goddess;
adorable young people in whom beauty was a tradition.   Some of them had complexions like wax,
others were as brown as mahogany; all alike had
that finished regularity of feature to which the
ardency or mildness of the eyes was but one detail
the more in a perfectly harmonious picture.   And
these beautiful creatures, at once placid and vivid,
were unconscious of their beauty, with the unconsciousness of animals; and they swarmed there like
animals, with a heartless and innocent delight in the
brutal details of those painted scenes of torture, in
which they saw their ancestors torturing their ancestors.   As they nudged one another, their eyes
glistening, and pointed to the saint who was being
boiled in a cauldron, the saint whose flesh was being
flayed off in long rolls, the female saint whose breasts

were being cut off with a long knife, I seemed to see
the true Roman mob as it had been of old, as it will
always be. It was just such people as these, with
their strong nerves, their indifference in the matter
of human life, who used to fill the Colosseum, as
simply as these filled the martyrs' church of San
Stefano Rotondo, when the martyrs themselves were
being thrown to the lions.

X

In a city laid out for the delight of the eyes it is
natural that much of the most intimate charm of the
city should linger in its villas and gardens, and there
is nothing which gives so much the sensation of that
mournful, yet not too mournful, atmosphere of partly
faded splendour which is the atmosphere of Rome as
the gardens of the Villa Mattei. Around are broken
walls rising brown and jagged against the sky, the
walls of the baths of Caracalla; a desolate strip of
country on the edge of the city; and beyond, seen
from the terraces lined with the dead bluish-
green of cactus, the Alban hills. All the garden
walks, where not even the cypresses are funereal
nor the sunlight itself gay, breathe an exquisite
melancholy, the most delicate and seductive breath
of decay. There are wandering terraces, slim vistas,
an entanglement of green and wayward life, winding
in and out of brown defaced walls fringed with ivy,

and about white and broken statues shining from under this green cloak of leaves; everywhere surprising turns of ways among the trees curving out here and there, as if instinctively, into a circle about a fountain, where broad leaves shadow the heads of gods or emperors in stone. And everywhere there is the cool sound of water, which rises in the fountains, and drips under water-plants in a grotto; and everywhere, as one follows the winding paths, a white hand stetches out from among the darkness of ivy, at some turn of the way, and one seems to catch the escaping flutter of white drapery among the leaves. You will sometimes see the shy figure of an old cardinal taking his walk there; and if you follow him, you will come upon a broad alley of ilexes, lined with broken statues, broken friezes, and arched over by fantastically twisted branches, brown and interlaced, on which the blue-gray leaves hang delicately like lace; an alley leading to what must once have been a sarcophagus, covered, on the side by which you approach it, with white carved figures. On the other side you find yourself in a little trellised circle, from which, as through a window suddenly opened, you see the Alban hills; there is a rustic wooden seat against the stone of the sarcophagus, on which, roughly carved, two lions meet and seem to shake hands; and above is written: "Qui San Filippo Neri discorreva coi suoi discepoli delle cose di Dio."

Just as I love the gardens of the Villa Mattei, so, for much the same reason, I love certain old churches and cloisters, which, hidden away in quiet corners, exhale, like a faint perfume, a sense of peace and of desolation in so singular a union. I am never tired of the Pace, the Church of Peace, which nestles against the Anima, the Church of the Soul, in a poor central part of the city. And it is not for the Sibyls of Raphael, admirable in grace of invention as they are, that I go to it, but partly for the frescoes of Baldassare Peruzzi, on the opposite wall, their stength, their gracious severity, their profound purity, and partly for something in the narrow compass, the dim colours, of the church itself, which seems to make it, not in name only, the Church of Peace. And in the midst of the Trastevere, with its high mouldering walls, its desolate open spaces, its yellow tortuous alleys, and half-fallen houses laid open against the road, one comes upon certain churches each of which has its own appeal. There is San Crisogono, Madame Gervaisais' church, big, rectangular, railed off from the world, with its vast dim emptiness, very restful as I have seen it at Vespers, mostly in shadow, a broad band of light showing, at one end, the white-robed priests, the dark shawls of old women, the children running to and fro over the floor, while one hears the pathetic little organ now before and now behind the voices which sing quavering responses. There is the basilica of Santa Maria in Trastevere, with its precious mosaics, standing aside from the yellow emptiness of the square. There is the church which had been the house of St Cecilia, in which you see the white plaintive marble figure of the martyr lying under the altar, in a delicate attitude, as if in sleep, with that ineffectual gash along the slim neck; the monastery with its little upper room in which St Francis of Assisi had lived, and where the old, half-blind, simple-minded monk shows you the famous portrait and the fragments of the saint's clothing. There is the monastery of San Cosimato, now an almshouse for old people, with its adorable unknown Pinturicchio, its august carved tombs underfoot, its mouldering cloister, in which precious marbles lie about like refuse; its ragged garden, which has grown green over one knows not what wealth of buried treasures; linen hanging to dry, old men and women moving slowly with bent backs: all this pathetic casual mingling of ruined magnificence and the decrepit old age of people living on charity, how expressive of Rome it is, and how curiously it completes one's sense of that desolation which is, as Shelley found it, "a delicate thing"!

And in all these rich churches in the midst of very poor people, all with at least their bit of precious marble, their fresco, their one fine picture, there is something which appeals to yet another sentiment; for, opening as they desire the gates of heaven to the poor, do they not certainly open the gates of that heaven on earth which is art? When I go into one of these churches and see how poor or humble or distressed people have come into them for the relief of rest, and when, as I sit there,

certainly with no devout thoughts, I feel the gradual
descent all around me of an atmosphere of repose,
which seems to shut one off, as with invisible wings,
from the agitations of the world, the busy trivialities
of one's own mind, all the little, active hindrances to
one's own possession of one's self, I realise how well
the Catholic Church has understood the needs of
that humanity to which she has set herself to
minister, and how medicinal a place she must always
have in the world's course, if no longer as a tonic,
still as the most soothing, the most necessary, of
narcotics.

XI

There are certain hours, there is something in
the aspect of certain places, churches, or gardens, in
which it seems to me that Bernini has interpreted
more of the soul of Rome than we are apt or anxious
to suppose. All that is florid, not quite sincere, un-
fairly spectacular, in the aspect of the city is summed
up for me in the four Doctors of the Church, in
black and white marble, who lean around the chair
of Peter in St Peter's, and in the ten loose-limbed
angels (done after Bernini's designs) who balance
themselves against an unfelt wind on the balustrades
of the Ponte Sant' Angelo. What is more subtle in
this same not quite sincere aiming after effect comes
out in the languid St Sebastian, in the church of
that name on the way to the Catacombs, his white

marble flesh pierced by gilt arrows, lying elegantly in his violent death; about which, indeed, the modern custodians of the church have set a whole array of painted card-board dolls, a very rag-fair. But subtler still, more intimately expressive of that part of the religious sentiment which must inevitably, in so ecclesiastical a city, come to complete, on the world's side, whatever is profane, sensuous, artificial, in the idea of devotion to the immaculate Virgin, is the Santa Teresa in the Church of S. Maria della Vittoria. The saint, who has the fine hands of a patrician lady, lies in an attitude of sharp, luxurious, almost active abandonment, the most sensual attitude I have ever seen in stone; her eyes are upturned, under their heavy lids, to where a stream of golden rays falls upon her, a new Danaë, while a young and smiling angel stands above her, about to pierce her heart with the arrow of divine love.

But if there are certain moods in which Bernini and his Rome seem to one the true Rome, there are others in which a deeper simplicity seems to indicate what is, after all, deeper in the heart of the city, as in some charming piece of unconscious poetry (superstition, if you like to call it so), such as the benediction of horses on the day of San Antònio Thaumaturgo. I love all superstitions, for I have never yet found one which did not come out of something which was once pure poetry. They are the people's heritage of poetry, and to believe them is to have, at all events, something of the mood, the mental attitude,

to which alone poetry can appeal. I spent some
time on the steps of the Church of San Eusebio on
that day of the benediction of horses, and I remember one very rough and wild-looking countryman
and his son, who drove up in a little homely cart, a
foal trotting by the side of the mare. The man got
down and waited, looking up anxiously, his cap in
his hand, until the priest came out with his card of
printed Latin and his gilt sprinkler, and blessed the
horses in the name of the Father and the Son and
the Holy Ghost; then the countryman put on his
cap with satisfaction, got into his cart, and drove off,
not knowing that he had been unconsciously living a
piece of poetry.

On another day, about Christmas, I saw the
Presepe in that church of the Aracœli (its altar
indeed near heaven) which has throned itself higher
even than the Capitol, upon which it looks down
from above its ladderlike steps, on which, if you see
them from below, people seem to be gliding down a
celestial staircase without moving their feet as they
pass from stair to stair. The lighted manger, as I
entered the dim church, was shown suddenly as the
sliding-doors were drawn back; and a priest, going
up into the midst of the painted dolls, took the
Bambino, a chubby red infant made of coarsely
daubed wood, his robes all golden and bejewelled,
out of his mother's arms, and carried him through
the church to the vestry, where he was held in front
of the altar to have his foot kissed. Women and

children crowded about him, smiling and pleased,
seeing what was droll, and at the same time the
poetry of the symbol. There I saw another side of
the religious element in Rome, the Christ of simple
women, of little children, as that sprinkling of the
horses had been the religion, centred in his beasts,
of the peasant, and the Bernini saint, in her ecstasy
of abandonment to the divine love, the patroness of
Roman boudoirs.

XII

In a toy-shop in the Via Nazionale there is on
one side a life-sized waxen clown dressed in red, who
winks his eyes, and taps with his hand on the
window ; on the other side is a little waxen clown,
seated, dressed in green, who holds on his lap a pig
with a napkin round its neck. He holds a piece
of meat in his hand, and the pig looks at it and puts
out its tongue. Then the clown shrugs his shoulders,
taps on the ground with one foot, and again holds
out the piece of meat to the pig, who licks it with
his tongue, when the clown again draws back the
piece of meat, shrugs his shoulders, and taps his foot
again. There never was anything more ingenious of
its kind, and every one who passes the window stops
in front of the two clowns and the pig. It seems to
me that in this puerile mechanical ingenuity I see
modern Rome as the Romans would like to make it,
as they have made it whenever they have had the

chance. That Rome should be a living city rather than a museum of antiquities is one of its special charms; and thus it is that Rome, in which all the ages are at home and jostle one another, is, more than any other city, a world in miniature. But Rome adapts itself less than most cities to all the unsightly economies and hurried facilities of modern progress. The Italian of to-day, the Italian in whose hands is the civic power, has resolved that his capital, which he knows to be the most historically interesting capital in the world, shall compete with all the young, pushing, commercial capitals on their own lines, which fortunately it can never do. He has set electric trams running past Trajan's Forum, and through narrow and crowded streets where they are an absolute danger. A little while ago he planned to surround the Forum with a gilt railing, but he had not the money to do it. He has put a hideous iron bridge across the Tiber close to the Ponte Sant' Angelo. He has built a gas-manufactory in the very midst of ancient Rome, and poisoned the air all round. He has cut down the secular cypresses of the Villa Ludovisi, and, indeed, all the trees he could lay his axe upon. But he has propped up every falling stone, and every stone is falling, of the house of the Anguillaras in the Trastevere, because Count Anguillara was the enemy of a Pope.

Modern Roman feeling, which, since the events of 1870, has been somewhat assertively patriotic, has certainly little sympathy for the Church. Has it, or

has it not, left the hearts of the people, remaining
but as a tradition a bowing of the head before the
passing of God, a lifting of the hat before the passing
of death? Are the priests, after all, making the
laws of a city which is in the hands of the enemy?
At all events, the Church is still able very im-
pressively to disregard what may be only a temporary
alienation. Walking one day from the Via Sistina
towards the Villa Medici, along that gracious height
which overlooks all Rome, and thinking of the very
temporal grandeur of what lay there before me, I
saw a young priest walking rapidly to and fro on the
flat roof of a house, his eyes fixed on his breviary,
never raising them to consider the splendour of the
city. He seemed to me to typify the serene, unthinking, and, because immaterial, invincible power
of the Church, throned there over what she does
not always even trouble to understand, so certain is
she that a power founded on faith is the master
of material things, and must always remain, even
in secret, even unacknowledged, even against men's
will, their master

XIII

What is subtlest in Rome must always reveal
itself to strangers, and not to the Romans; for the
modern Roman is given over to the desire and
admiration of material things, and what is subtlest
in Rome appeals to the soul, perhaps I should say,

rather, to the mind. Since I have lived in Rome I have come to find both London and Paris, in themselves, a little provincial; for I find them occupied with less eternal things, or with less of the immediate message of eternal things speaking in them, than this liberating Rome. Rome, properly apprehended (and to apprehend it properly it needs only that you are not without a certain intelligence, and that you remain passive to your impressions), seems to shut one in, as with its own walls, upon the greatest moments that have been in the world; upon the greatest moments of art, of history, of religion, of humanity. It is not merely that they are there; you cannot escape them. Every road does not lead to Rome, but every road in Rome leads to eternity. It is quietly prodigal of itself, like the air about one, which is part of one's breath. In this large Rome one has room for one's self; within these walls one is shut in from others, and from what in one's self is the reflection of their image; one's energies are not torn into little ineffectual pieces, as they are in the rapid drawing this way and that of the daily life of all other great cities. One has time to discover that while there are many interesting and even intoxicating things in the world, there are very few things of primary importance. It is like the opening of a great door. This opening of a door, in front of which one has passed constantly without even seeing that it was shut, is the moment for which every other moment in life was but an unconscious

waiting; every moment which follows will remember it. For the most part this door is but
opened and· then shut suddenly, before our eyes
have become well accustomed to the unfamiliar
light in which we discern, it may be, familiar objects.
It is not often that the door is held steadily open as
long as we choose to look through it. But that is
what happens in Rome.

In London I am too close to a multitude of interesting trifles, of attractive people, of opportunities
for the satisfaction of every desire. To will and to
receive are, in London, simultaneous. Daily life is
too importunate in thrusting upon me whatever for
an idle or perverse or estimable moment I have
hankered after. There are too many people, too
many books, too many museums, too many theatres;
the spectacle of this feverish, unslackening life is
too absorbing. I cannot escape the newspapers;
for even if I do not read them, there is always some
one to tell me what they have been saying of
my own or my friend's last book. I cannot help
sometimes asking myself what will be the immediate,
urban effect of something which I have written;
and it is a little humiliating to find one's self in so
trivial a mental attitude, which it would be difficult
to preserve in front of the Pantheon or of the
Colosseum. And, above all, I have not time to live.
Life scatters into waves all over the rocks, falling
back broken and dispersed into the seething trouble
of the ocean. Yesterday is to-day, and to-day to-

morrow, before I have been alone with myself for an hour. That canopy of smoke which London has set up between itself and the sky imprisons me, day by day, with the débris of each day. I forget that anything else exists.

In Paris, frankly, I am too much at home, too happy; I require too little; life is too easy, and answers too readily to the demands of the senses. And Paris, which frees me from one conventionality, imposes upon me another. Because the flesh is an honourable part of the human constitution, and liberty an honourable prerogative of the citizen, it does not follow that a permissible exemption should become a precept, a very prejudice. And that is just the provinciality of that bright, youthful, inspiriting, and seductive Paris which I love so much, and in which I find it, after all, more nearly possible to be myself than in London ; for Paris is not merely the city of the senses, but the city of ideas, the ideas of pure reason.

But Rome has freed me from both these tyrannies, the tyranny of the senses and of the ideas of pure reason. It neither absorbs me too much in material things nor forces me into too rapid mental conclusions. So much of the world's history lies about here, in these stones, like a part of nature, and with so far more significant a meaning than in the mere picturesque heaping of natural forces. Empires have lived and died here; the great spiritual empire of the Western world still has its seat upon the seven hills ; here are all the kingdoms of art ; and is it possible to find anywhere a more intimate message than in these voices, in this eloquent Roman silence ?

WINTER, 1896.

VENICE

The Grand Canal at Venice.
From an Engraving after the Picture by J. M. W. Turner.

VENICE

I

COMING in the train from Milan, we seemed, for the last ten minutes, to be rushing straight into the sea. On each side was water, nothing but water, stretching out vaguely under the pale evening light; and at first there was not a sign of land ahead. Then a wavering line, with dark ships, and thin shafts of rigging, came out against the horizon, like the first glimpse of an island; the line broadened, lights began to leap, one after another, out of the darkness, and a great warehouse, glowing like a furnace, grew up solidly out of the water. We were in Venice.

I had never been in Venice before, and in the excitement of the moment I resolved that I would find my way to St Mark's on foot, through the labyrinth of streets and bridges, in which I did not even know whether to turn to the right or to the left, for I had lost my guide-book in changing trains at Bâle. It seemed to me amusing to trust myself to the attraction of the centre, and I set out confidently, following as far as I could the main stream of people. I walked fast, plunging deeper and deeper into unknown ways, which were like

nothing I had ever seen, turning now to right, now
to left, crossing the bridges, with their long, low
comfortable steps, seeing the black flash of a
gondola round a sudden corner, under me, and down
the vanishing waterway between tall houses with
carved balconies and stone steps rising out of the
water; turning down narrow alleys, where two
people could only just walk abreast, alleys which
broadened all at once into great empty squares,
a rococo church in one corner, a fifteenth-century
palace in another, then a wider alley, in which
bright crowds were buying and selling out of
brilliantly coloured shops, women in vivid shawls,
walking superbly, men in beautiful rags lounging
against the wall and lying in doorways; then
another grey square, a glimpse, in the opening
between two houses, of gondolas lying in the water,
between the tall stakes of a ferry; and then again
the narrow and dim alleys. I went on and on,
turning back, trying another alley, and still the
endless alleys seemed to reach out before me, and
the bright crowds grew thinner and thinner: endless! and was I really going farther and farther
away? I began to wonder, and I turned back, half
way up a narrow street, and asked the way to the
Piazza. Straight on, they told me, up that very
street, a few steps; and all at once, going a few
steps beyond the point at which I had turned back,
I found myself suddenly free of all that coil of
entangling alleys, which had seemed to be tighten-

ing about me like a snake; I came out into a great
space, seeing for the first time a clear breadth of
sky, and there, against the sky, was St Mark's.

I was glad to see Venice for the first time by
night, and to come into it in just this casual fashion.
A place has almost the shyness of a person, with
strangers; and its secret is not to be surprised by
a too direct interrogation. A guide-book is a
necessary evil; but it is not when I have had a
guide-book in my hand that I have received my
lasting impressions. I have spent weeks in the
churches of Venice, climbing upon ladders, and
propping myself against altars, and lying on my
back on benches, to look at pictures; and I have
learnt many things about Tintoretto, and Bellini,
and Carpaccio, and Tiepolo, which I could have
learnt in no other way. But what I have learnt
about Venice, Venice as a person, has come to me
more or less unconsciously, from living on the
Zattere, where I could see the masts of ships and
the black hulls of barges, whenever I looked out
of my windows on the canal of the Giudecca; from
sitting night after night outside a café in the
Piazza, listening to the military band, watching
people pass, thinking of nothing, only singularly
content to be there; from strolling night after
night down to the promontory of the Dogana, and
looking into the darkness of the water, watching
a man catching fish in a net like a shrimping net,
while the sound of the mandolins and of the

voices of singers who sat in lantern-lighted gondolas outside the windows of the hotels on the Grand Canal came to me in a double chorus, crossing one another in a strange, not inharmonious confusion of tunes; and especially from the Lido, that long, narrow bank between the lagoon and the Adriatic, to whose seaward side I went so often, merely to be there, on the sand beyond the bathing-huts, watching the quietude of the sea. On the horizon there would be a long, tall line of fishing-boats, their red sails flashing against the pearl grey of the sky like the painted wings of great moths, spread for flight; as you gazed at them, they seemed to stand there motionless; then, as you looked away for a moment and looked back again, one of them would have vanished suddenly, as if it had gone down into the sea. And the water, which rippled so gently against the sand at my feet, had something of the gentleness of colour of that water which wanders about the shores of Ireland. It shone, and seemed to grow whiter and whiter, as it stretched out towards the horizon, where the fishing-boats stood up in their long, tall line against the sky; it had the delicacy, the quietude of the lagoon, with, in those bright sails, the beckoning of a possible ˜escape from the monotony of too exquisite things.

II

Venice has been sentimentalised by the German
and by the young lady of all nations.   Lovers have
found its moonlight and its water more expressive
than the moonlight and the water of any other shore.
Byron, Musset, Wagner, Browning, have lived and
died there.   It has been painted by every painter.
It has become a phrase, almost as meaningless as
Arcadia.   And indeed it is difficult to think of
Venice as being quite a real place, its streets of
water as being exactly real streets, its gondolas as
being no more than the equivalent of hansoms, its
union of those elsewhere opposed sentiments of the
sea, the canal, the island, walled and towered land,
as being quite in the natural order of things.   I had
had my dreams of Venice, but nothing I had dreamed
was quite as impossible as what I found.   That first
night, as I looked at the miraculous, many-coloured
façade of St Mark's, the pale, faintly-tinged marble
of the Doge's Palace, I seemed, after all, not to have
left London, but to be still at the Alhambra, watching a marvellous ballet, and, as it pleases me to
be, in the very midst of it, among the glittering
"properties," knocking at every step against some
fragment of delicately unreal scenery, losing none of
the illusion by being so close to its framework.   The
Doge's Palace looked exactly like beautifully painted
canvas, as if it were stretched on frames, and ready

to be shunted into the wings for a fresh "set" to come forward. Yes, it is difficult to believe in Venice, most of all when one is in Venice.

I do not understand why any one paints Venice, and yet every one who paints, paints Venice. But to do so is to forget that it is itself a picture, a finished, conscious work of art. You cannot improve the picture as it is, you can add nothing, you need arrange nothing. Everything has been done, awaits you, enchants you, paralyses you; the artistic effect of things as they are is already complete : it leaves, or should leave you, if you have artistic intentions upon it, helpless. Mere existence, at Venice, becomes at once romantic and spectacular : it is like living in a room without a blind, in the full sunlight. A realist, in Venice, would become a romantic, by mere faithfulness to what he saw before him. People are always saying in Venice, "What a picture that would make!" but the things of which people say that are just the things in which nature, time, art, and chance have already made pictures, have already done all that the artist should be left to do for himself : they remain for the photographer. The only chance, it seems to me, for the artist in Venice is to realise frankly, that, in this water which seems to exist in order that it may set off the delicacy and slimness and fine decoration of architecture which on land would appear to have lost the key of its harmony, in this architecture which seems to have grown up out of the water in order that it may be

a flower on the surface of the water, he is painting
the scenery of a masque or ballet.

And yet, after all, but perhaps it will only deepen
your impression of that unreality which is Venice,
the masque or ballet, you will soon find, is over.
The scenery is still there, the lights have been left
on ; only the actors, the dancers, are gone. That is
one element of the melancholy, which is an element
in the charm of Venice; but a certain sadness is
inherent in the very sound and colour of still water,
and a little of the melancholy which we now feel
must always have been a background of shadow,
even at the most splendid moment of the masque.
Now, when art and commerce, the Doges and the
galleys, have alike drifted into the past ; when the
great squares are too large for the largest crowds
that are ever to be found in them, and the great
palaces, too large for their owners, are passing into
the hands of Jews and Americans ; when the tracery
of Renaissance windows looks out between broken
glass and roughly fixed boards, and the balustrades
of balconies moulder and wear away under the
dripping of clothes hung over them to dry ; when
this city of carnivals and masked balls, Goldoni's,
Longhi's, is asleep by midnight, it may well seem
as if silence and desolation have descended on it like
a cloud. Why is it then that the melancholy of
Venice is the most exquisite melancholy in the
world ? It is because that melancholy is no nearer
to one's heart than the melancholy in the face of a

portrait. It is the tender and gracious sadness of
that beautiful woman who leans her face upon her
hands in a famous picture in the Accademia. The
feast is over, the wine still flushes the glass on the
table, the little negro strikes his lute, she listens to
the song, her husband sits beside her, proudly :
something not in the world, a vague thought, a
memory, a forgetfulness, has possessed her for the
moment, setting those pensive lines about her lips,
which have just smiled, and which will smile again
when she has lifted her eyelids.

III

All Venice is a piece of superb, barbaric patch-
work, in which the East and the West have an
equal share. The lion of St Mark's, his head and
shoulders in one piece, his hind-quarters in another,
is a symbol of the construction of Venice, just as
the bronze horses, which have seen the downfall of
Nero, the splendours of Constantinople, and, at
Paris, the First Empire, are a symbol of its history.
Venice is as near to the East as it is to Italy ; you
are reminded of the East at every step; yet, after
all, its interest is precisely that it is not Eastern,
that it is really of the West, and that it has given a
new touch of the fantastic to the fantasy which we
call Oriental, an arrangement of lines and colours
which, in its own country, has a certain air of being

at home, but which, out of its country, frankly
admits itself barbaric, a bastard.

In the thirteenth century there was a law which
obliged every Venetian merchant, coming back from
a voyage, to bring with him something for the
adornment of the basilica. Thus it is that St Mark's
has come to be one vast mosaic, in which every
piece of marble is itself a precious thing, perhaps
brought from the other end of the world, and a kind
of votive offering. The church is like an immense
jewel, a piece of goldsmith's work, in which the
exquisite and the fantastic are carried to so rare a
beauty, in their elaborate mingling, as to attain
almost to a perfection in spite of themselves. Unlike
other great churches, the beauty of St Mark's is not
so much structural as in ornament, ornament which
seems, indeed, to become a part of its very substance.
It is not for its proportions, for the actual science
in stone of a Palladio or a Sansovino, that it comes
to be, in a sense, the most beautiful church in the
world, but because it has the changing colours of an
opal, and the soft outlines of a living thing. It
takes the reflection of every cloud, and, in certain
lights, flushes into a rose, whitens to a lily. You
enter, and your feet are upon a pavement which
stretches away in coloured waves like a sea; over
your head is a sky of pure gold, a jewelled sky, in
which the colours and the patterns are the history
of the whole world. The gold, when the light
strikes it, glitters in one part like rock-crystal, in

another like gilt chain armour.   Rosy lights play
upon it, and the very vault dies away in soft fire.

Yet St Mark's has nothing of the spiritual mysti-
cism of a Gothic cathedral, any more than it has
the purely ecclesiastical atmosphere of St Peter's.
It is half temple, half mosque; it has the severity of
an early Christian church, overlaid by the barbaric
splendours of the East; and its splendours, too, are
hieratic, in a strange and fantastic hierarchy which
seems to partake of all the religions, the beginnings
of Christianity seen visibly building themselves up
out of the ruins of Paganism; and the rites of the
Greek Church or of the Catholic would be equally
in place.   It is a church which is also the world, a
little world into which everything enters; where
everything that has human beauty, or curiosity, or
value, is not too beautiful or valuable, and could in
no way be unsuited, for the divine use.   And St
Mark's has room, still, for all the world and all the
churches.   Tourists walk about carrying red guide-
books, and listening to the chatter of guides; old
people, with handkerchiefs over their heads, twisted
like turbans, kneel with clasped hands and unconscious eyes; the High Mass goes on in the choir,
invisibly, behind the great barrier, through which
there comes the sound of voices chanting; and, in a
side chapel, an old priest says his Mass to a few
devout persons.   And nothing seems out of place, the
devout persons, the priests, the tourists, the largest
onyx in the world, over the pulpit, the profane

sumptuousness of African marble, the "majestical
roof fretted with golden fire"; for here, as everywhere in Venice, all contradictions seem able to exist
side by side, in some fantastic, not quite explicable,
unity of their own.

IV

High Mass at St Mark's, as I have seen it at
Easter and at the feast of St Mark, is somewhat less
magnificent a ceremony than in most churches; for
the elevation and seclusion of the choir permit the
sight of the holy mysteries only to the few who can
find room inside the screen, or in one of the side
chapels, or in the galleries. The galleries, indeed,
give much the best point of view. Looking down
from that height, you see the priests move through
their appointed courses, the vestments, the incense
mounting on the wings of the music, among the
voices; and the great crowd crawling over the
pavement, with a continual motion, from the church
to the Piazza, from the Piazza to the church, settling
down, now and again, into solid groups, like the
pigeons outside. And indeed the aspect of the
church is very similar to the aspect of the Piazza.
It has the same air of space and leisure; it can be
thronged, yet never appears to be full, and it has the
same air of belonging to the people. On a festa
everybody comes in, as naturally as everybody walks
up and down the Piazza; there is the same bright

crowd, face for face, shawl for shawl. It is not an instinct of devotion; it is habit, and the attraction of the centre. In Venice all roads lead to the Piazza, and the Piazza is but the courtyard of St Mark's.

The Piazza di San Marco always gives one an impression of space; yet, put into Trafalgar Square, how much room it would leave over! The buildings on three sides of it, though of different dates, and of very different interest as architecture (part of the south side being the Library of Sansovino, the finest public building in Italy), are all perfectly regular, and, at a general view uniform; yet there is no sense of monotony, but rather of a distinguished precision, which, in its rich severity, is somehow more various than variety itself. And the Piazza, with its arcade of shops and cafés, though it is in one sense the Rue de Rivoli of Venice, the resort of every foreigner, is still, as it always has been, the resort of the people, and of all the people. The Englishman or the German, though he takes his ice at Florian's, or his coffee at the Quadri, like a native, is, after all, only an outside spectator of the really Venetian way of taking one's leisure. The first time I came into the Piazza, on an afternoon when the band was playing, I saw what seemed to me either a wedding or a funeral. A procession was slowly making its way along, a procession which seemed interminable; and, on coming nearer, I found that in effect it never ended, for the line returned upon itself like the winding line of a farandole, and while those nearer to the Procuratie Vecchie were always coming from the direction of St Mark's, those farther out were always going towards it. The order was rarely broken, and the incredible slowness of the step was never quickened. It was the public promenade, in which only the costumes have changed, century after century; not the faces, nor the step, nor the drawling line returning upon itself, in which all Venice, shawled, bare-headed, bourgeois, aristocratic, and the carabinieri, imposing, ornamental creatures who seem for once in their place, in such a procession, take the air together. Another leisurable crowd darkens the *terrasse* of the cafés, spreading far out into the Piazza from under the arcades; and around the bandstand in the middle there is yet another crowd, standing attentively, while the band plays the eternal Verdi, the eternal Ponchielli; and about them, wings wide in the sunlight, the pigeons come swooping down, each with his little pink feet poised delicately, close together, separating just as they touch the ground. At night the same promenade goes on: but the pigeons are sleeping, among the carved angels and beside the bronze horses of the basilica. Under the gaslight and the clear, dark blue of a sky which seems stretched like the silk of a velarium, the winding line is denser than ever. Little groups are clustered in every corner, on every step, on the pedestals of the flagstaves, on the marble slabs of St Mark's, between the porphyry columns, on the marble bench in front of the Loggetta. At ten the crowd begins to melt away; by eleven,, only Florian's and the Quadri have still their gay, chattering disputants, little set by little set, each in its own room, or on the chairs outside it. But there are still lingerers about the flagstaves, before the Loggetta, and in the doorways and arches of St Mark's; bare-headed women and children, half asleep, their bright shawls drawn round them, lounging so beautifully, in such coloured outline, and with such a visible sense of repose.

V

The main thoroughfare of Venice, the street of shops, which leads from the Piazza everywhere, is the Merceria, which you enter under the clock-tower, on which the two bronze gentlemen strike the hour with their hammers. After many windings it broadens out, just before reaching the Rialto, into the Campo San Salvatore, and from that onwards to the Campo San Bartolommeo. From Good Friday to Easter Monday there is a sort of little fair here, and stalls are set up under the church of San Salvatore, and all around the little railing within which stands Goldoni's statue. He stands there, looking down on the people as if he saw in them one of his comedies; firmly planted, wearing his court dress with an air, and with an intensely self-satisfied smile of amused interest on his face. If he could only turn his head, he would look right up the steep, broad stairs of the Rialto, which lie there to the right, bright with moving crowds of colour, winding up and down on each side of the central line of stalls, between the shops, hung with long coloured stripes. He stands there, looking down on the people. All around are tall grey houses, with shutters of green and pale blue; one house, in a corner, has shutters of an intense blue, which seems to soak up and cast back all the sunlight. The stalls are but a few boards, hastily set up on trestles; they are hung with bright rows of stockings, necklaces, toys, heaped with sweets, and shirts, and shawls; some of them are old book-stalls, piled with worthless books in all languages, mostly in calf, together with numerous little works of gallantry and devotion, all in paper; there is a *Fonografico Excelsior*, and there are glittering copper things, pots and pans, lying all over the ground; and there is a pentagonal kiosque of unpainted wood, with little flags flying, and paper placards stuck across it, at which two women in striped blouses, aided by a man, are serving out endless tiny cups of coffee, at a halfpenny a cup. The cry of " Acqua ! " is heard at every moment, and the water-carriers pass, with their framework of glasses and their covered copper pans of water. The men, who stand or sit by the stalls, are all smoking. Sometimes they take the cigar from

their mouths to shout their wares, but for the
most part they seem indifferent to purchasers;
especially one old and dirty Jew, with long hair
and a long beard, who puffs placidly at his pipe
as he watches the stall of cheap kerchiefs to which
no customer ever comes. I noticed particularly a
group of five old women, with turbaned heads and
a century of wrinkles, and another group of eleven
facchini and beggars, some of whom were very
old men, with tattered, yet still dignified cloaks,
huge brigandish hats, their bright red stockings
showing like an ornament through the gaps in their
boots. They were terribly dirty; but in Venice,
where everything has its own way of becoming
beautiful, dirt, at the right distance, gives a fine
tone to an old face, like those faces that we see in
the sketches of Michelangelo, wrinkled like a
withered apple, tanned to a sombre red, and set
in the shadow of long grey hair and beard. Dirt,
on such a face, a kind of weather-stain, has that
dignity which dirt, in England, gives to an old
ruin. Here the old ruin is the beggar-man, and
he is not less picturesque, not less dignified, than
any castle in England.

VI

A part of Venice that I like, not because it is
attractive in itself, but because it is so unlike the
show Venice and so like a fishing village, with its

smell of the sea and ships, is the Via Garibaldi, which runs from Veneta Marina past the Public Gardens. It is a broad thoroughfare, which I can look up and down for some distance, a rare thing in Venice ; and I have often sat here, intently idle, watching every one who passes me. All that is humbler, more truly indigenous, in Venice, seems to pass, at one time or another, along that highway between the two main branches of the lagoon, the shore which looks towards San Giorgio, the Riva, and the shore which looks towards Murano, the Fondamenta Nuova. Sailors are always passing, and fishermen, with their heavy heelless shoes, and fine ruddy-brown knitted stockings, ribbed in circular coils, which they wear like top boots ; the faces here are bronzed to a deeper tone of red than in any other quarter except the Giudecca. Sometimes a company of soldiers comes marching past, in their dark blue great-coats and helmets, their drab trousers and gaiters ; they walk briskly, with the swinging gait of the Italian soldier.

The houses are old, and mostly white, with green and brown shutters which have faded from the crudeness of their original colours, to become a soft lilac, a delicate chocolate. There are a few booths in the middle of the road, under the little starved trees, laid out for the most part with clothes, skirts and handkerchiefs, and fruit ; the two necessities of existence here, bright-coloured things to wear, and fruit to eat. A *facchino* is lying flat on his face, asleep, on one of the polished marble benches, his vivid blue trousers glittering in the heat of the sun; another *facchino* leans against a tree, smoking; men, women, and children are lying along the walk, basking in the sunlight; some of the children are bare-footed, for the people about here are a little more sordid in their poverty than in most parts of Venice, though without that air of depression which I have noticed in the Canareggio quarter. Two little red-shawled children are sitting on a seat opposite to me, counting their treasures; groups of small people, carrying just slightly smaller babies, are resting against the entrance to the gardens. I hear at every moment the slip-slop of heelless shoes dragging their way along the pavement, and catch a glimpse of the heels of brilliant stockings, red, striped, white, occasionally a fine, ecclesiastical purple; now a whole flock of greenish yellow shawls passes, then, by itself, a bright green shawl, a grey, a blue, an amber; and scarcely two of all these coloured things are alike: the street flickers with colour, in the hot sunshine. Italian women are never at rest in their shawls, they are always unwinding them, resettling their folds, shifting them from head to shoulders, and back again, slipping out a ringed hand to sketch a whole series of gestures. And they are never in a hurry. They come and go, stop, form into groups, talk leisurely, and then go on their way, almost, I like to think, with the

mechanical movement of a herd of cows, with the
same deep sense of repose, of animal contentment,
which comes of living in the sun.

VII

Venetian women are rarely pretty, often charming, generally handsome. And all of them, without
exception, walk splendidly, not taking little mincing
feminine steps, but with a fine, grave stride, due
partly to the fact that they are accustomed to wear
heelless slippers, which oblige them to plant the feet
firmly, and the whole foot at once, without a chance
of tripping upon the toes or pounding upon the
heels, as women who wear tight boots are able, and
only too apt, to do; they walk with almost the same
action as if they were bare-footed, and almost as
well. And they use the whole body in walking,
not with the undulatory motion of Spanish women,
but with a movement of the whole back and
shoulders, in the exact swing of the stride. Venetian women do, however, remind one in many ways
of Spanish women, in their way of doing the hair,
of wearing the mantilla, for instance ; the Moorish
element, which is their bond of union, coming out
so naturally in Venice, where one finds, quite as a
matter of course, an *Antico Caffè dei Mori*, where a
cigarette is still known as a *spagnoletto*, where the
dialect touches Spanish at all points. The types of

Venetian women vary in every quarter: the women of the Castello have quite a different look from the women of the Dorsoduro. In a seaport town there is always a certain intermixture of races, and Venice, with the different layers of its different occupations and conquests, is variable to a greater degree than most seaports. Remembering that nearness which Venice has always had to the East, it is not altogether surprising to find among the Venetian types, and not least frequently, one which is almost Japanese. They are singularly charming, these small, dark, cat-like creatures, with their small black eyes, vivid as the eyes of a wild animal, their little noses, prettily curved in at the tip, their mouths, with thick, finely curved lips, their hair, too, sometimes drawn back in the Japanese manner. And they have that look of cat-like comfort and good-humour, which is also a Japanese habit. Then there are many Jews here, and in the Jewish women you find often the finest type of Jewish beauty, in which the racial characteristics stop short just at the perfect moment. You find, too, but only now and again, the vivid swarthiness of the gipsy, with the gipsy's shining black hair, as black and polished as ebony, plaited and coiled tightly round the back of the head.

Then there are many quite blonde women. The Venetian red does not, indeed, exist, if it ever did, in nature; the recipes for its production may still be read: a painful process, in which you sat in the full

heat of the sun, with your face covered, and your
hair laid out around you to get soaked and coloured
with sunlight. The women nowadays feel that the
colour is not worth the headache. But they add to
nature in one matter with extraordinary persistence :
they powder their faces, slightly on week-days, and
thickly on festas, rarely with much art, with, rather,
an ingenuous obviousness which, so far as my
observation goes, is unique. Even quite young
girls use *poudre de riz*, without the slighest necessity
for its use ; possibly, for one reason, because they
think it bad for the complexion to wash the face
much, and powder saves a good deal of washing.
It gives a charming air of sophistication to people
who are not too civilised to be frankly human, who
are in most things so natural and who are so happily
wanting in those "little ways" which we call, by
way of reproach, feminine. But they are full of
fantastic contradictions, powdering their faces, which
are nice, and leaving their figures, which are sometimes inclined to broaden unreasonably to take care
of themselves, without the aid or the direction of
stays. And there is something elaborately artificial
in the way many of them have of doing their hair,
in little kiss-curls, composed in all manner of different
ways ; in little rows of cork-screws, or harebells
tinkling along the forehead; or in trails down
the side of the cheeks, as in Carpaccio's great
picture of the "Courtesans." There is something, in their whole aspect, slightly self-conscious,

F

charmingly so, indeed; a *smorfia* which gives a curious, ambiguous, at once asking and denying complaisance to their lips and eyes, as if they refused nothing without a full knowledge of what they were refusing. Women and girls, even children, dress exactly alike; and there is nothing more comical, more charming, than the little people of twelve who look like twenty; brilliant, fascinating little people, at once very childish and very mature, with their hair coiled at the back like their elders, their skirts down to their heels, their shawls too long for them, dangling to the ground, but worn with an air of infinite importance and self-sufficiency. And the colours of all these women, the elegant olives, the delicate blondes, the sombre browns, are thrown out so admirably, so finely adorned, by the vivid colours of shawls, and dresses and stockings, which would be gaudy elsewhere, but which here, in the heat and glitter of such an atmosphere, are always in place, never immoderate. They are all part of the picture, the great *genre* picture which is Venice.

VIII

Spectacular as all Venice is, there is nothing in all Venice more spectacular than the gondola. It is always difficult for me to realise that a gondola is not a living thing. It responds so delicately to a touch, the turn of a muscle; is so exquisitely

sympathetic, so vivid in its pride of motion, so gentle
and courteous with an adversary. And just as a
perfect rider becomes one body with his horse,
realising actually the fable of the centaur, so the
gondolier and the gondola seem to flow into a single,
human rhythm. Nor is the gondola an easy
creature to master. To poise yourself on the edge
of the stern, and row forward, using only half a
rowlock, and to shoot round corner after corner,
from a narrow canal into a narrower, without so
much as grazing the prow of the gondola which
meets you : that requires, at every moment, the
swift and certain address of the polo-player guiding
his pony through a crashing mêlée. I never quite
knew whether it was more delightful to lie in a
gondola and watch the land from the water, or to
watch the gondola from land. From land, perhaps,
at night, when something slim and dark glides by,
the two rowers moving in silhouette, with the
fantastic bowing motion of the little figures at the
Chat Noir ; or, again at night, when you hear a
strong voice singing, and a coloured line floats down
the canal, the singing boat in the midst, paper
lanterns tossing a variable light over the man who
stands at the prow, and the women with hooded
heads, smiling, who play an accompaniment on
mandolins. But from the water, certainly, if it is
your good luck to see a great *serenata*, such as the
one I saw when the King of Italy and the Emperor
of Germany played that little masque of Kings at

Venice.   The *galleggiante*, with its five thousand
lights, a great floating dome of crystals, started from
the Rialto; from the midst of the lights came music,
Wagner and Rossini, Berlioz and the vivid, rattling,
never quite sincere, *Marcia Reale*; and the luminous
house of sound floated slowly, almost imperceptibly,
down the Grand Canal, a black cluster of gondolas
before it and beside it and behind it, packed so tightly
together that you could have walked across them,
from shore to shore.   From my gondola, in the
midst of all these black hulls and bristling steel
prows, through the forest of oars, upright in the
water, between the towering figures of the gondoliers bending against their oars, over the heads of
the mass of people heaped together on this solid,
moving, changing floor of boats, I could see a yet
greater crowd on every point of the shore, on the
steps of the Salute, along the line of the Dogana,
on every landing-stage, at every window, high up on
the roofs.   Bengal lights burned steadily, flash-
lights darted across the sky, with their crude,
sudden illumination; rockets went up, paper lanterns
swayed and smoked; and as we floated slowly, imperceptibly down, it seemed as if the palaces on each side
of us were afloat too, drifting past us, to the sound of
music, through a night brilliant with strange fires.

  What struck me then, as I found myself in the
midst of this jostling, tightly packed crowd, every
gondolier in violent action, shouting in that hoarse,
abrupt, stomachic voice which goes so well with the

unconsonated Venetian dialect, was that not a single
one of them lost his temper, though each was doing
his best to outwit the other, and get his gondola a little
nearer to the music; and I reflected how much the
situation would have tried the temper of a London
cabman. Their language, like their gestures, was
but decorative. The gondolier in Venice is as fine
to look at as his gondola; he has colour, too, in the
ruddy dye of his face, the infinite variety of his amber
shirts and blue trousers and scarlet sashes; and if
you really know him, he is one of the most charming
of people. It is by no means knowing the gondoliers
to have known them only as a master who hires a
man, and gets him at the lowest bidding. Living
on the Zattere, near which so many of them live, I
have had the chance of seeing them as they are
among themselves; I have played *boccie* with them in
the bowling-alley under the trellised vines, from
which the first drops of sap were beginning to drip;
I have sat with them in the tavern parlour, beside the
great chimney-corner, under the burnished pots and
pans, watching them play a mysterious game with
fantastic cards. And I have always felt myself to be
in the company of gentlemen.

IX

Goldoni, in his memoirs, tells us that the Venetians
sang all day long, "the shopkeepers laying out their

wares, the workmen coming home from work, the gondoliers waiting for their masters "; and he adds : " Gaiety is at the root of the national character, and jesting is at the root of the Venetian language." The day is past when the gondoliers sang Tasso, and the shopkeepers do not sing now; but they stand at the doors of their shops and smoke, and, like everyone else in Venice, take things comfortably. *Il dolce far niente* is a sensation which can scarcely be realised more completely than in Venice ; and with such a sky, such water, and such streets, who would look for a bustling race of business people, like the Milanese ? In Venice no one will work very hard for the sake of " getting on " : why should he ? I never saw poor people who seemed so happy, and who were really so comfortable in their poverty, as the very poorest people here. The softness of the climate, the little on which the comforts of life depend, permit poverty, even beggary, to remain dignified. Simply to lie in the sun, to have just enough to eat, and plenty of cheap cigars to smoke : a poor man demands little more than that, and it is rare indeed that he does not get so much. Time scarcely exists in Venice ; it certainly does not exist for the idle poor. They hanker after no luxuries ; for, in Venice, merely to live is a luxury. Think of a city where bread and wine, fruit and flowers, are the chief things hawked about the streets ! Wherever you go you hear the cry of " Acqua ! " you see a basket heaped up with brilliant flowers, and not far off some one is lying asleep, *a facchino* in vivid blue, one wooden shoe under his head for a pillow, stretched at full length in any nook of shade. More even than in Rome, scarcely less, and far more agreeably, than in Naples, the whole place belongs to the people. The beggar who curls up asleep on your doorstep has an equal right with your own, and, so far as the doorstep is concerned, a greater; for you do not require it to sleep on, and he does. And there is scarcely an inch of Venice where he cannot lie down and go to sleep whenever he likes. Streets where a horse or cart is unknown are so surprisingly clean, comfortable, and leisurely; they are made to be loitered in, lain upon, and for every man to have his way with. The moral of "The Sick King in Bokhara,"

> "That, though we take what we desire,
> We must not snatch it eagerly,"

needs no enforcement in Venice. Every one takes what he wants; but he takes it gently, gracefully, as a matter of course. Your cigars belong to your gondolier as much as to yourself; and if he has two oranges, one of them is yours.

The Venetians have but few amusements. There are four theatres, and these are only open for a few months out of the year, and supported only by strolling companies; there is a theatre of marionettes open still more rarely; and that is all. Once upon a time there was a café-chantant,

with a little company from Vienna: Annie Vivanti
has sung there; but it has dwindled almost out
of existence; and there is not a music-hall or
a public dancing-hall in the whole city. No doubt
this is partly because the people are so poor that
they cannot pay for even the cheapest amusements,
but is it not, also, because they do not require
them, finding sufficient pleasure in things as they
are, in the mere quiet gaiety of daily life, the fact
of living always in the midst of a *décor de théâtre*,
of which they are themselves acting the drama?
That animal content which comes over one in
Venice, taking away the desire of action and the
need of excitement which way-lay the mind and
the senses under less perfect skies, makes it just
as possible to be happy without running after
amusement, as the simplicity of the conditions of
life makes it possible for the poor man to live on
polenta and a little fruit. There is something
drowsy in the air of Venice, as there is something
a little sleepy in the eyes of the Venetians. Is
not life, to those who live there always, as it is
to those who come and go in it for pleasure, a
kind of day-dream?

Spring, 1894 and 1897.

NAPLES

Naples and Bay.
From a photograph by Brogi.

NAPLES

I

I HAVE rarely entered a strange city without a certain
apprehension; but no city ever filled me with such
terror as Naples. Those long streets of tall, mean
houses, from which narrow alleys climbed the hill,
and descended to the harbour, in row after row of
meaner and not less tall houses, all with their little
iron balconies, over which clothes and linen draggled,
all with their crowded, squalid, patched, and coloured
throngs of restless life; the cracking of whips, the
clatter of wheels and of horses' hoofs on the uneven
stones; the thud of the cow-bell, the sharper tinkle
of the goat-bell, as the creatures wander about the
streets or wait at the doors of houses; the rattling
of bootblacks' brushes, the petulant whine of beggars,
the whole buzz of that humming, half-obliterated
Neapolitan, with its punctuation of gestures; the
rush and hustling of those side-walks, after the
ample and courteous leisure of Rome; something
sordid in the very trees on the sea-front, second-
rate in the aspect of the carriages that passed, and
of the people who sat in them; the bare feet, rags,
rainbow-coloured dirt, sprawling and spawning poverty
of Santa Lucia, and not of Santa Lucia alone; the

odour of the city ; and then the indiscoverable length and extent of it, the ways that seemed to lead in whatever direction I wanted to go, and then ended suddenly, or turned aside in another direction ; the darkness up the hill, and the uncertainty of all those new, as yet unknown, roads: that, as I turned away from the sea, when night began to come down upon it, mounted to my head like some horrible fume, enveloping me with disgust, possessing me with terror. I have got a little accustomed to it now, I know my way through those streets, which are, after all, simple enough in their arrangement; I have come to see certain advantages, even, in the turning of all this dirt and poverty out into the sun ; I find it a touching tribute to cleanliness that every other poor person whom you see is hunting for his own or his neighbour's vermin ; but, all the same, I think my first impression is likely to last.

I do not think that the Neapolitans are more vicious or intend to be more objectionable than other people, but they are poor, naturally untidy ; they live in the street because there is sun and air in the street, and it does not occur to them that there is anything in human nature to hide. They have an absolute, an almost ingenuous, lack of civilisation, and after seeing the Neapolitans I have more respect for civilisation. I am not convinced that the whole of the pavement belongs to the dirtiest part of the people who walk on it, and that these have exactly the right to encamp with their wives and families in the way of one's feet, and to perform quite the whole of their toilet before one's eyes. For these people, whom you see in Santa Lucia and the Strada del Porto and along the whole of the quays, are as shameless as animals: look into their faces, and you will see in their great, dark eyes the unintelligent regard of animals. Old age and infancy are here more horrible than anywhere else; that beginning and ending of human life in helplessness and physical dishonour are here emphasised with all the cruelty of which nature, left to herself, is capable. A Christian ascetic, wishing to meditate on the disgust of the flesh, might well visit these quays. There he will see the flaccid yellowness of old women, like the skin of a rotten apple; wrinkles eaten in with grime, until they broaden into ruts; feet and ankles that have been caked and roasted and soaked into iridescent reds, smoky violets, shot purples; the horror of decayed eyes, deformed limbs, hair crawling with lice; and about these dishonoured bodies flutters a medley of blackened and yellowing linen, tattered trousers without buttons, tattered dresses without strings, torn shawls, still loud in colour, but purple where they had been red, and lavender where they had been blue. And all this malodorous medley is a-swarm, hoarse voices crying, hands in continual movement, the clatter of heelless shoes on the pavement, the splash of emptied vessels, laughter, the harsh notes of a song, rising out of their midst like the bubble of steam escaping out of a boiling pot.

II

Naples varies in aspect according as you see it from above or below, from the side which looks towards Vesuvius, the side which looks towards Capri, the side which merges into Posillipo; and no generalisation can express the effect of this precipitous and straggling town, under the shadow of the burning mountain, and itself crawling up and down the sides of volcanic hills, set in a half-circle against the curve of the bay. Looking from Capodimonte you would say that it nestled among green trees; looking from the sea-front you would say that it was built out of the sheer rock. And its colour varies like its contour. Rain warmed by sunshine brings out the finest colours, and shows you the roofs and railed and windowed walls in their most effective groupings, house piled above house, like rock piled above rock, green foliage seeming to grow out of their crevices. There never was a town which seemed to have been so little made, to have grown so entirely according to its own whim, and with so little regard to any consideration but the crowding of houses into every available inch of ground, street intersecting street, and *salite, scale, rampe* rising out of these intersections wherever an unfilled corner could be found. Looking down on the side streets of Chiaia and Toledo is like looking down the clefts in a rock, the crevices of a mountain side; looking up

them, to the glimpses of the hill above, is like looking
up from the bottom of a gorge. And whenever you
climb, by stairways or winding terraces, to a certain
height, you see on the east the double ridge of
Vesuvius, smoke coiling into clouds above the crater,
its sides, in clear weather, spotted white with houses,
in dull weather an indistinguishable mass of violet or
purple, like the colour of thunder-clouds; on the
south, the bay, in which Capri and the ridged coast
of Sorrento appear and disappear with every change
of weather, like the stains in stone, or a picture
which the magic-lantern flashes upon and away from
the sheet.

III

Naples has ceased to be merely horrible to me, a
boiling pot; it has become a witches' cauldron. I
begin to be fascinated by those streets which are
corridors, with their violent shadows, their obscure
exuberance of life; those strange glimpses, as I
climb at night through terrace after terrace of sordid
streets, the houses open to view, the one large room
lit with the smoking oil-lamp, the figures bending
over it, the white beds set side by side, from one of
which you see already the nightcapped head of the
grandmother, or a child's tumbled black hair; vague
figures still leaning into the darkness from their
balconies, now and then the sudden descent of a
basket at the end of a string, the sound of a man-

dolin or piano organ, a song, or the rattle of feet on
the floor; for the most part silence, or a low chatter
which does not reach me. Lights shine out suddenly
from curtained windows, doors open and shut, you
hear the bolts drawn. And all kinds of strange
archways, passages, steps leading up or down, indefinite turnings, perplex one at every step. There
is a crucifix which I pass every night; it is only a
crucifix painted upon wood, but it is set up in a
shrine like the gable of a house, there are five oil-
lamps about it, which cast singular lights on the
suffering figure, hanging there, as if on a Calvary, at
the side of the pavement, with fresh flowers at its
feet. That, too, seems to me like something not
quite natural, a part of the same sorcery which has
piled all these rocky ways and set up these cavernous
houses. No, there never was a town so troubling,
so disquieting, so incalculable as Naples, with its
heavenly bay lying out in front for strangers to gaze
at, and all this gross, contentedly animal life huddled
away in its midst, like some shameful secret.

IV

Wherever I go in Naples, in the streets, the
theatres, the churches, the cafés, I see the same
uncouth violence of life, the same ferment of un-
civilisation. Occasionally, when two Neapolitans
meet in the street, they kiss one another with a
loud kiss; for the most part they do not shake

hands, they do not nod, they do not lift their hats; they stare fixedly, with an expression which I took to mean violent aversion until I came to find it indicated extreme friendship. Watching from a little distance a group of men at a café table, you cannot tell whether they are or are not having a serious altercation. When a Neapolitan gesticulates he does it with all his fingers and the whole of his face; when he does not gesticulate, he is rigid. All that is best, certainly, but all that is most typical in the Neapolitan seems to me to be summed up in the writer who more than any other has given in literature the whole savour of Naples. Matilde Serao makes on one the impression of a good-humoured gnome. Full of strength, sincerity, emotion, full of an irresistible charm of humanity, she is so short and stout as to be almost square; her head, too, with its low forehead, is square; and she sits humped up, with her head between her shoulders, all compressed vivacity, which is ready to burst forth at any moment in a flood of energetic, humorously emphatic words, to which her leaping gestures with her short fat fingers, in front of her nose, of her grimacing eyes, of her cheeks wrinkled with laughter, add a further and a yet more grotesque emphasis.

I heard the " Cavalleria Rusticana " one night at the San Carlo theatre, and, though the character of the music is properly Sicilian, it seemed to me to have a good deal in it of the people among whom it is so popular. This crackling music, a fire which

G

crackles out, has an acute, feverish, quite Southern sentimentality, the sentimentality of the mandolin and the knife. Kindling, certainly, while you listen to it, it is wiped out, as a sponge wipes out figures on a slate, with the first breath of air you draw outside. And the true, canaille, Neapolitan music, the Piedigrotta songs and the rest, which you hear all day long, shouted, whistled, played on piano-organs, on mandolins, in the streets, in the restaurants, in the cafés-chantants, have they not the very odour of the streets in them? The songs are often enough obscene, as popular songs often enough are, and to hear Emilia Persico or Maldacea sing them, with a knowing vivacity, an abominable languor, is to realise all that they are capable of in the way of significant expression. But in the tunes themselves, with their heady notes, their pauses and rushes, their careful uncertainties of rhythm, their almost Spanish effects of monotony, there is something at once greasy and fiery, an acrid vulgarity which stings the senses, revolting and depraving, with a kind of intoxication like the intoxication of cheap wine.

At Easter the Neapolitans mourn for the death of Jesus Christ as the Greeks mourned for the death of Adonis. It is a sacred play to them, in which they take the same turbulent, and, for the moment, absorbing interest, as in an opera at San Carlo, or a melodrama at the Mercadante. On Good Friday, during the " Tre Ore " of the Passion, I went into the popular central church of Santa Trinità Maggiore.

Between the high altar and the pulpit, where a
queer, black figure in his cornered hat preached
with a sounding voice and the gestures of a puppet,
there was a rough platform, draped with blue cloth,
on which was an orchestra of black-coated gentlemen
and some singers, who sang with high Mascagni
voices. The people, coming in continuously by
twos and threes, rushed about the church as if it
were the market-place, precipitately, greeting their
friends with little sharp hisses of recognition, turning
about in their chairs, chattering in whispers, waving
their hands to one another, standing and arranging
one another's hats. Never have I seen such bustling,
restless, disorderly churches, or people so un-
civilised in their devotions. During the "three
hours" the church was packed in all its corners,
people sitting on the altar-steps, and on the altars,
perched in and around all the confessionals; the men
piled their hats into the empty holy-water basins,
the women who had come without hats did not cover
their heads with handkerchiefs; during the sermon
all listened attentively, as to a really absorbing play.
On the day before Holy Thursday, there had been
the celebration of the Santo Sepolcro. The doors
of the churches were draped in black, the high
altar was covered with black cloth, and on a black
cloth before the high altar the crucifix was laid out,
as if in a tomb. Some of the Christs were small, of
dark metal, almost indistinguishable from a little
distance; others were large, made of painted wood,

with smears of red paint for the five wounds; and a
crowd came and went all day long, mostly women,
and these women knelt and kissed the five wounds,
almost prostrating themselves on the floor. There
was something grotesque, familiar, amorous, extravagant, in this unending procession of women, rich
and poor, young and old, all, one after another,
dropping on their knees, leaning over the sacred
body, whose passion was shown to them with so
visible a significance; something, I cannot tell what,
barbaric, infantile, sensuous, in the sight and sound
of all those devout and eager kisses, which they
gave with a passionate solemnity, as to a lover.

V

Outside Naples, between Vesuvius and the sea,
half-buried and half-recovered from the earth, the
ghastly suburb of Pompeii repeats, like a remote
echo, the very note of Naples. Pompeii, though
you will find it large enough when you follow all
the intersections of its abrupt, crossing ways, remains in the memory like a toy city, or a cabinet in
a museum. And, as one walks in these streets, in
which noise or silence is alike oppressive, interrupt-
ing, it is possible to persuade oneself that one is
merely visiting a museum, looking at curiosities. In
so frightful a step back of nearly twenty centuries,
the mind reels, clutching at that somewhat pacifying

thought, for at least its momentary relief. And
then, all at once, turning aside into an empty street
from the guide and the visitors, you are seized, and,
as it were, imprisoned within the terror of this
image of the immortality of death, before which all
the legends of hell become credible, seeing how
hard it is to escape, even by death, out of the bond-
age of even a material indestructibility. Here are
the bodies of men and women, moulded for ever in
the gesture of their last moment, and these rigid,
earthly corpses are as vivid in their interrupted life
as the wet corpses lying on the slabs of the Morgue,
the suicide of yesterday. These hastily set up walls
might have been built last year, and the rut of the
waggon-wheels in the solid pavement of lava is like
a wheel-mark left overnight in the dry mud of a
country road. The brothel and the temple are here,
side by side, and here, only just cleansed from its
burial, is a villa, its walls still bright with paint, still
eloquent with frescoes, the little bronze and marble
images still smiling about the fountains and flower-
beds of the central garden ; a pot, the yellow rust
of lava corroding it, set over the fire which went out
suddenly on that twenty-fourth of August, A.D. 79.
Feeling the stone and mortar of these jerry-built
walls, noting the conventional glibness of these
graceful decorative paintings, realising, by the very
signs of its "pleasant sins," that here, after all, was
but the Brighton of its day, you seem, by the consciousness of all that is trivial, temporary, accidental

in it, to be brought closer to that so strangely
capricious survival of ancient death.   And then,
going out into the road, in the first step beyond the
hedge, in the first breath of relief at the sight of
the little station, the two hotels for visitors, the
quiet fields in which men are digging, fruitful fields
stretching out to the roots of the mountains all
around, Vesuvius smoking placidly above, this un-
bearable sense of the nearness of life suspended so
many years ago drops back suddenly, and again it is
as if it had never been, and again you have persuaded
yourself that this is after all only a show in a
museum, a collection of curiosities, a toy city which
had never really had anything too intimate to do
with humanity.

VI

There is in Naples the image of a world, which
adds a new world to one's contemplation, not less
vivid and swarming than those streets; and that
world of the Aquarium seems as real, as natural, in
all its fantastic, extravagant, and enigmatical life, as
the life of human beings.   It is, indeed, first by its
humanity that it strikes us, by the strange irony of
the likeness which one sees in these scaled, pulpy,
and many tentacled creatures of the sea, in the very
expression of their eyes and bodies, and also in the
whole manner of their occupations among the rocks
and their neighbours, with the faces and the doings

of men. There is not a human vice or absurdity
which I have not seemed to see in these drowsy, and
irritable, and rapacious, and surly, and pre-occupied
creatures, their whole lives spent in catching flies
(with what an elaborate mechanism of means to that
end!) in coiling and uncoiling an army of suckers to
the very obliteration, almost, of the centre of their
being; in fanning themselves, with soft, unresting
wings, forwards and backwards, forwards and backwards, for ever, neither turning nor ceasing for a
moment. Some have the aspect of eternal age, as
others have the curse of eternal activity. In the
great, sullen, flat creatures with their purple bodies,
their bull-dog jaws, their heavy eyes, I see the gross
bourgeois, as he is everywhere in the world; it
seems that he inhabits the water as he inhabits the
earth, and with the same authority. Is there not a
heavy coquetry in the motions of a certain kind of
eel, the very effervescence of bumptious youth in
the little fishes with fins which look like arms
akimbo, the very parody of our aspirations in the
diaphanous, delicately coloured creatures, edged
with lavender, who have puffed all their life into
their heads, which for ever pant and strain upwards
like balloons, as if trying to free themselves of the
little tangle of body still left to them? Then, too,
there is a fantasy more terrible than any nightmare,
a soft, seductively coloured, deceptive, strangling
life in these clinging, and absorbing, and stealthy
apparitions of the sea, which come and go in the

water with the sudden and soft violence of the water itself.

Coming up out of the twilight, where I have been gazing into the glass boxes filled with water, wondering at these uneasy miracles of the sense of touch, I find myself replunged into the bustle of Naples, for the concert has begun in the Villa, and people are walking to and fro under the trees, and sitting on the chairs about the band-stand, listening to the harsh din of those brass instruments playing their noisy, military, Italian music The garden of the Villa Nazionale lies for a mile along the sea front, from the Largo della Vittoria almost to the beginning of Posillipo, and you can stand under the curdling blossoms of the Judas trees, and still see the blue water shining under the afternoon sun or the tossing of the little waves when the wind begins to blow them grey. On the afternoon when I had visited the Aquarium, clouds began to climb over the top of the hill, catching stormy colours and then turning leaden ; and presently the concert came abruptly to an end, as the rain poured with a straight, steady violence, scattering the people hither and thither into the little wooden cafés, under the thin branches of trees, under the drooping hoods of cabs, and behind the flapping curtains of trams. I sat in one of the cafés and watched the hurry of people unprepared for anything but sunshine ; the blind rush through the puddles, the shelterless lingering under dripping trees, the half-desperate, half-hoping glances upward at the grey sky, which might be blue again at any moment, or perhaps not for an hour's time. All the brightness, the unconsidering gaiety, of Naples had gone out like a candle in the wind ; life seemed to come angrily to a pause, in this sudden hostility of nature. Presently I heard the twanging of a string : two men with mandolin and fiddle were standing in the doorway, and a woman began to sing one of the Piedigrotta songs. A man carrying a cloth-covered box came in, took off his cap, and went smilingly, persistently, from table to table with his tortoise-shell combs, his corals, and his brooches of lava. Outside the window crouched a dark, handsome, half-witted beggar-girl, with her red handkerchief over her head, her white teeth shining in a smile ; she held out her little brown hand, beckoning for alms ; and standing there, bare-footed in the rain, seemed to bring back the Neapolitan accent to Naples.

Spring, 1897.

SEVILLE

The Giralda Tower, Seville.

SEVILLE

I

SEVILLE, more than any city I have ever seen, is
the city of pleasure. It is not languid with pleasure,
like Venice, nor flushed with hurrying after pleasure,
like Budapest; but it has the constant brightness,
blitheness, and animation of a city in which pleasure
is the chief end of existence, and an end easily
attained, by simple means within every one's reach.
It has sunshine, flowers, an expressive river, orange-
groves, palm trees, broad walks leading straight into
the country, beautiful, ancient buildings in its midst,
shining white houses, patios and flat roofs and vast
windows, everything that calls one into the open air,
and brings light and air to one, and thus gives men
the main part of their chances of natural felicity.
And it has the theatres, cafés, shops, of a real city,
it is not provincial, as Valencia is; it is concentrated,
and yet filled to the brim; it has completely
mastered its own resources. Life is everywhere;
there are no melancholy gaps, vacant spaces, in
which a ruinous old age has its own way desolately,
as in most really picturesque cities; as in Venice,
for instance, which it resembles in so many points.
It has room for itself, and it is not too large for

itself. And in living gaily, and in the present, it is carrying on a tradition: it is the city of Don Juan, the city of Figaro.

I am coming, more and more, to measure the charm of cities, at all events their desirability for living in, by the standard of their parks, public gardens, and free spaces where one can be pleasantly unoccupied in the open air. I want the town, not the country, but I want the town to give me the illusion of the country, as well as its own characteristic qualities. Rome itself, without its villas, even Rome, would not be Rome; and Seville, which is so vividly a town, and with so many of a town's good qualities, has the most felicitous parks, gardens, and promenades (with that one great exception) that I have ever found in a city. Gardens follow the riverside, park after park, and every afternoon Seville walks and drives and sits along that broad road leading so straight into the open country, really a Paseo de las Delicias, a road of trees and sunlight. Turn to the right or to the left, and you are in a quiet shadow, under lanes of orange trees and alleys of acacias. There are palms and there is water, and there are little quaint seats everywhere; paths wind in and out, roses are growing in mid-winter, they are picking the oranges as they ripen from green to gold, and carrying them in the panniers of donkeys, and pouring them in bright showers on the ground, and doing them up into boxes. Great merchant vessels lie against the riverside, unloading their cargoes; and across the park, on the other side of a wall, drums are beating, bugles blowing, and the green meadow-grass is blue and red with soldiers. In the park, girls pass wrapped in their shawls, with roses in their hair, grave and laughing; an old gardener, in his worn coat with red facings, passes slowly, leaning on his stick. You can sit here for hours, in a warm quiet, and with a few dry leaves drifting about your feet, to remind you that it is winter.

Seville is not a winter city, and during those months it seems to wait, remembering and expectant, in an acquiescence in which only a short and not uneasy sleep divides summer from spring. To the northern stranger, its days of sunshine and blue sky seem to make winter hardly more than a name. Sun and air, on these perfect winter afternoons, have that rare quality which produces what I should like to call a kind of active languor. The sharpening of a breath, and it would become chill; the deepening of the sunshine, and it would become oppressive. And just this difficult equilibrium, as it seems, of the forces of summer and winter, adds a zest to one's contentment, a kind of thankfulness which one does not find it needful to feel in the time of summer. How delightful to sit, perfectly warm, under a tree whose leaves are scattered about the ground, yellow with winter; to watch the bare branches, among these always green palms and orange trees, re-membering winter in the North.

But to enjoy sympathetically all that Seville, even

in winter, can be to its own people, it is not enough
to go to the parks and the Paseo; one must go, on
a fine Sunday afternoon, to the railway line which
stretches onwards from the Barqueta, along the
riverside, but in the opposite direction. The line is
black with people, at one hour going, at another
hour returning, an unending stream which broadens
and scatters on both sides, along the brown herbage
by the river, and over the green spaces on the
landward side. At intervals there is a little venta,
there are bowling-alleys, swings, barrel-organs,
concertinas, the sound of castanets, people dancing,
the clapping of hands, the cries of the vendors of
water, shell-fish, and chestnuts, donkeys passing
with whole families on their backs, families camping
and picnicing on the grass, and everywhere chairs,
chairs on the grass, two sitting on each chair, in a
circle about the dancers, as they dance in couples,
alternately; chairs and tables and glasses of manzanilla
about the ventas; and always the slow movement
of people passing, quietly happy, in a sort of grave
enjoyment, which one sees in their faces when
they dance. Here is the true *pueblo*, the working-
people, *cigarreras*, gipsies, all Triana and the
Macarena; and could people amuse themselves
more simply or more quietly, with a more en-
joyable decorum? As they turn homewards, in
another long black line, the sun is setting; a
melancholy splendour burns down slowly upon the
thin trees across the water, staining the water with

faint reflections, and touching the dreary, colourless shrubs along the river-side with delicate autumn colours, as sunset ends the day of the people.

II

There are seven hundred streets in Seville, and there is hardly a street which has not some personal character of its own, or which does not add one more line to the elaborate arabesque of the city. One of my favourite aspects, for it is an aspect from which Seville looks most Eastern, is at just that point of the Paseo de Catalina de Rivera where it is joined by the Calle San Fernando. One sees the battlemented outer wall of the Alcazar, with its low, square towers, the Giralda, the brown turrets of two or three churches, and then nothing but white walls and brown roofs, with a few bare branches rising here and there delicately against the sky, between the sharp, irregular lines of the houses, all outlined in bright white. One can fancy a whole Kremlin or Hradčin clustered inside that low, white, battlemented wall; outside which the dreary Paseo, and the dim green of the Prado San Sebastian, seem to be already the country.

And it is from this point too, as one turns homeward from the river-side, that evening seems to come on most delicately: those sunsets of blue and rose and gold, as the sun goes down across the

H

Guadalquivir, and that rosy flush which encircles all
Seville after the sun has gone down, as if the city
lay in the hollow of a great shell, tinged with rose
at the edges. It is at just this hour that Triana
looks its best, heaped somewhat irregularly on
the other bank, in a long, white and pink line, above
the brown slime ; and from the Triana bridge, always
crowded with lean, beaten horses, dragging too
heavy loads, and lines of white donkeys with panniers,
nodding their jingling heads, as they wander along
by themselves, one sees the whole river, and the
Moorish Tower of Gold, and the crowded masts,
changing colour as the light changes moment
by moment.

The streets of Seville are narrow, for shade in
the summer and warmth in the winter, and many
of them, like the central Calle Sierpes, with its
shops, and clubs, and cafés, a street of windows,
are closed to wheels. Every house has its balconies,
and the older ones their barred windows on the
ground floor ; and every house has its patio, that
divine invention of the Moors, meant, certainly, for
a summer city, and meant, as one sees it in Morocco,
for houses without windows, in which all the light
comes from the open roof above an inner court.
The Spaniards have both patios and windows, for
summer and winter, in their wise, characteristic
passion for light. All the doors, leading to the
patio, are of open iron-work, no two doors alike,
in their surprisingly varied, and often exquisite,

arabesques of pattern. This throwing open of one's house to the street, yet with an iron door, always closed, setting a boundary to the feet if not to the eyes, seems to me again characteristic of these natural, not self-conscious people, who seem often so careless of their own dignity and liberty, and are so well able to preserve them.

Seville lights up for a feast-day as a face lights up with a smile. The night before the great feast of the Immaculate Conception, I went into the streets to find the whole place transformed, glittering. Crimson or white and blue cloths were thrown over balconies, rows of lamps and candles burned above them, and between the lights eager faces leaned over, looking down at the eager faces looking up at them. The public squares were brilliant with light, and the whole place became suddenly filled with people, passing to and fro in the Sierpes, and along the streets of shops, which I hardly recognised, so brilliantly lighted were all the windows. The transformation seemed to have been done in a minute, and here was the true Seville, idle, eager, brilliant, moving gaily, making the most of the world on the Church's terms of felicity for the other world.

And yet this, if the true Seville, is not all Seville, and I found another, silent, almost deserted city, which fascinated me almost more than this living and moving one, whenever I wandered about at night, in streets that sank to sleep so early,

and seemed so mysteriously quiescent, under the
bright sky and the stars. Night passed rarely
without my coming out of some narrow street
upon the vast Plaza del Triunfo, which holds the
Cathedral, its Pagan counterpart, the Giralda, the
Alcazar, and the Lonja. The tall tower of the
Giralda was always the first thing I saw, rising up,
like the embodied forces of the delicate powers
of the world, by the side of the Christian Cathedral.
Seen from the proper distance, it is like a filigree
casket that one could lift in the hand, as Santa
Justa and Santa Rufina lift it, in Murillo's picture;
looking up from close underneath it, it is like a
great wall hiding the stars. And the Moors have
done needlework on a wall as solid as a Roman
wall; far finer work than that bastard splendour
of the Alcazar, with its flickering lights, and
illuminations like illuminations on parchment.

Looking back at the Giralda and the Cathedral
from the gateway of the Patio de las Banderas,
one sees perhaps the finest sight in Spain. The
Giralda stands motionless, and a little aloof; but
by its side the vast, embattled magnificence of the
Cathedral seems to change in every aspect, full
of multiform life, ordered to a wonderfully expressive variety, throwing out new shoots in every
direction, like a tree which grows into a forest in
some tropical country, or like a city grouping itself
about a citadel. It is full of the romantic spirit,
the oriental touch freeing it from any of the too

heavy solemnity of the Middle Ages, and suiting it to a Southern sky. Above all, it has infinitely varied movement: yes, as it seems to lean slightly from the perpendicular, all this vivid mass might be actually about to move, to sail away like a great ship, with all its masts and spread sails and corded rigging.

III

Much of what is most characteristic in the men of Seville may be studied in the cafés, which are filled every evening with crowds of unoccupied persons, who in every other country would be literally of the working class, but who here seem to have endless leisure. They are rough-looking, obviously poor, they talk, drink coffee, buy news-papers and lottery tickets, and they are all smoking. They fill rows of tables with little companies of friends; they are roughly good-humoured, affection-ately friendly with one another; and their conversa-tion echoes under the low ceiling with a deafening buzz. The typical Andalusian, as one sees him here, is a type quite new to me, and a type singu-larly individual. He is clean shaved, he wears a felt hat with a broad flat brim, generally drab or light grey, clothes often of the same colour, and generally a very short coat, ending where a waist-coat ends, and very tight trousers; over all is a voluminous black cloak lined at the edges with crimson velvet. He is generally of medium height, and he has very distinct features, somewhat large, especially the nose; a face in which every line has emphasis, a straight, thin, narrow face, a face without curves. The general expression is one of inflexibility, the eyes fixed, the mouth tight; and this fixity of expression is accentuated by the arrangement of the hair, cut very short, and shaved around the temples, so as to make a sharp line above the ear, and a point in the middle of the forehead. The complexion is dull olive, and in old age it becomes a formidable mass of wrinkles; by which, indeed, many of these old men with their clean-shaved cheeks, bright eyes, and short jackets, are alone to be distinguished from their sons or grandsons. There is much calm strength in the Andalusian face, a dignity which is half defiant, and which leaves room for humour, coming slowly up through the eyes, the mouth still more slowly lengthening into a smile; room also for honest friendliness, for a very inquiring interest in things, and very decided personal preferences about them. Often the face runs all to humour, and the man resembles a comic actor. But always there is the same earnestness in whatever mood, the same self-absorption; and, talkative as these people are, they can sit side by side, silent, as if in brooding meditation, with more naturalness than the people of any other race.

The Andalusian is seen at his finest in the bull

fighter, the idol of Seville, whom one sees at every
moment, walking in the streets, sitting in his club,
driving in his motor car, or behind his jingling team
of horses, dressed in the tight majo costume, with
his pig-tail drawn up and dissimulated on the top
of his head, his frilled shirt with great diamond
studs, his collar clasped by gold or diamond fasten-
ings, diamond rings glittering on his well-shaped
fingers. I once sat opposite one of the most
famous toreros at a *table-d'hôte* dinner, and, as I
contrasted him with the heavy, middle-class people
who sat around, I was more than ever impressed by
the distinction, the physical good-breeding, something almost of an intellectual clearness and shape-
liness, which come from a perfect bodily equipoise,
a hand and eye trained to faultless precision.

The women of Seville are not often beautiful,
but one of the most beautiful women I have ever
seen was a woman of Seville whom I watched for an
hour in the Café America. She had all that was
typical of the Spaniard, and more ; expression, the
equivalent of a soul, eyes which were not merely
fine, but variable as opals, with twenty several
delights in a minute. She was small, very white,
with just that delicate hint of modelling in the
cheeks which goes so well with pallor; she had
two yellow roses in her black hair, at the side of
the topmost coil, and a yellow shawl about her
throat. One wished that she might always be
happy.

More often the women are comfortable, witty, bright and dark, *guapa*, rather than beautiful; almost always with superb hair, hair which is like the mane or tail of an Arab horse, and always with tiny feet, on which they walk after a special, careful way of their own, setting down the whole foot at each step, level from heel to toe, and not rising on it. In Seville, more than anywhere else, one sees the Spanish woman already mature in the child, and nothing impressed me more than these brilliant, fascinating little people, at once natural and conscious, with all the gestures of grown women, their way of walking, their shawls, and, in their faces, all that is finest in the Sevillana, a charm, seductiveness, a sort of caressing atmosphere, and not merely bright, hard eyes, clean-cut faces, animation, which are to be seen everywhere in Spain. They have indeed that slightly preoccupied air which Spanish children affect, and which deepens, in some of the women, into a kind of tragic melancholy. Pass through the Macarena quarter in the evening, and you will see not the least characteristic type of the women of Seville: strange, sulky, fatal creatures, standing in doorways, with flowers in the hair, and mysterious, angry eyes; Flamencas, with long, ugly, tragic, unforgettable faces, seeming to remember an ancestral unhappiness.

There is a quality which gives a certain finish to Spanish women, and which is unique in them. It is a sort of smiling irony, which seems to penetrate the whole nature : the attitude of one who is aware of things, not unsatisfied with them, decided in her own point of view, intelligent enough to be tolerant of the point of view of others, without coquetry or self-consciousness ; in fact, a small, complete nature, in which nothing is left vague or uneasy. It is a disposition such as this which goes to make life happy, and it is enough to have watched the gay, smiling, contented old women to realise that life is happy to most women in Spain. Look in all these faces, and you will see that they express something very definite, and that they express everything, while Northern faces have so much in them that is suggestion, or, as it seems to the Spaniard, mere indefiniteness. The Southern nature, for its material felicity, has retained the Pagan, classic ideals ; the Northern has accepted the unquiet, dreaming soul of the Middle Ages.

But in Spanish women, along with much childishness and much simplicity, there is often all the subtlety of the flesh, that kind of secondary spiritual subtlety which comes from exquisitely responsive senses. This kind of delicacy in women often stands in the place of many virtues, of knowledge, of intellect ; and, in its way, it supplies what is lacking in them, giving them as much refinement as knowledge or the virtues would have done, and itself forming a very profound kind of intelligence. I recognise it in the mournful pallor, and that long, immobile gaze, which seems to touch one's flesh, like a slow caress ;

that cold ardour, which is the utmost refinement of fire. And these white people carry themselves like idols. Singularly different is that other Spanish kind of animality, where life burns in the lips, and darkens the cheeks as if with the sun, and bubbles in the eyes, the whole body warm with a somewhat general, somewhat over-ready heat. It is enough to have heard the laughter of these vivid creatures. It is the most delicious laughter in the world; it breaks out like a song from a bird; it is sudden, gay, irresponsible, the laughter of a moment, and yet coming straight from the deep unconsciousness of life. The Spanish woman is a child, but a mature Spanish child, knowing much; and in the average woman of Seville, in her gaiety, humour, passion, there is more than usual of the childlike quality. Their faces are full of sun and shadow, often with a rich colour between Eastern and Western, and with the languor and keenness of both races; with something intoxicating in the quality of their charm, like the scent of spring in their orange groves. They have the magnetism of vivid animal life, with a sharp appeal to the sensations, as of a beauty too full of the sap of life to be merely passive. Their bodies are so full of energy that they have invented for themselves a new kind of dance, which should tire them into repose; they live so actively to their finger-tips that their fingers have made their own share in the dance, in the purely Spanish accompaniment of the castanets. A dance is indicated in a mere shuffle of the feet, a snapping of the fingers, a clapping of hands, a bend of the body, whenever a woman of Seville stands or walks, at the door of her house, pausing in the street, or walking, wrapped in many shawls, in the parks; and the dance is as closely a part of the women of Seville as their shawls, the flowers in their hair, or the supplementary fingers of the fan.

IV

A significant quality of the Andalusians is the profound seriousness which they retain, even when they abandon themselves to the most violent emotions. It is the true sensuality, the only way of getting the utmost out of one's sensations, as gaiety, or a facile voluptuousness, never can. The Spanish nature is sombre and humorous, ready to be startled into vivid life by any strong appeal: love, hate, cruelty, the dance, the bull-fight, whatever is elemental, or touches the elemental passions. Seeing Seville as I did, in winter, I could not see the people under their strongest, most characteristic intoxication, the bull-fight; but I had the opportunity, whenever I went into the street, and saw a horse dragging a burden, of seeing how natural to them is that cruelty which is a large part of the attraction of bull-fighting. And their delight in violent sensations, sensations which seem to others not quite natural, partly perverse, partly cruel, as in the typical emotion of the bull-fight, is seen at Seville in the "cuerpo de baile infantil" which dances at the Café Suizo. These children of ten or eleven, who dance till midnight, learned in all the contortions of the gipsy dances, which they dance with a queer kind of innocence, all the more thorough in its partly unconscious method, and who run about in front, sitting on men's knees in their tawdry finery, smiling out of their little painted faces with an excited weariness; is there not a cruelty to them, also, in the surely perverse sentiment which requires their aid in one's own amusement? I shall never forget one particular dance of two children, one of the most expressive gipsy dances, danced in trailing dresses, inside which, as inside some fantastic, close prison or cage, they hopped and leaped and writhed, like puppets or living tops, to the stupefying rattle of castanets; parodying the acts of physical desire, the coquetry of the animal, with an innocent knowingness, as if it were the most amusing, the most exciting of games. One of them was a little, sallow, thin creature, with narrow eyes and an immense mouth, drawn almost painfully into a too eager smile; a grimacing, Chinese mask of a child, almost in tears with nervous excitement, quivering all over with the energy of the dance. I went to see them, indeed, frequently, as I should have gone to see the bull-fights, and with the same mental reservation. They reminded me of the horses.

All Spanish dancing, and especially the dancing of

the gipsies, in which it is seen in its most characteristic development, has a sexual origin, and expresses,
as Eastern dancing does, but less crudely, the
pantomime of physical love. In the typical gipsy
dance, as I saw it danced by a beautiful Gitana at
Seville, there is something of mere gaminerie and
something of the devil; the automatic tramp-tramp
of the children and the lascivious pantomime of a
very learned art of love. Thus it has all the excitement of something spontaneous and studied, of vice
and a kind of naughty innocence, of the thoughtless
gaiety of youth as well as the knowing humour of
experience. For it is a dance full of humour, fuller
of humour than of passion; passion indeed it mimics
on the purely animal side, and with a sort of cold-
ness even in its frenzy. It is capable of infinite
variations; it is a drama, but a drama improvised
on a given theme; and it might go on indefinitely,
for it is conditioned only by the pantomime, which we
know to have wide limits. A motion more or less,
and it becomes obscene or innocent; it is always on
a doubtful verge, and thus gains its extraordinary
fascination. I held my breath as I watched the gipsy
in the Seville dancing-hall; I felt myself swaying unconsciously to the rhythm of her body, of her
beckoning hands, of the glittering smile that came
and went in her eyes. I seemed to be drawn into a
shining whirlpool, in which I turned, turned, hearing
the buzz of the water settling over my head. The
guitar buzzed, buzzed, in a prancing rhythm, the

gipsy coiled about the floor, in her trailing dress,
never so much as showing her ankles, with a rapidity
concentrated upon itself; her hands beckoned,
reached out, clutched delicately, lived to their finger-
tips; her body straightened, bent, the knees bent
and straightened, the heels beat on the floor, carrying
her backwards and round; the toes pointed, paused,
pointed, and the body drooped or rose into immobility,
a smiling, significant pause of the whole body. Then
the motion became again more vivid, more restrained,
as if teased by some unseen limits, as if turning upon
itself in the vain desire of escape, as if caught in its
own toils; more feverish, more fatal, the humour
turning painful, with the pain of achieved desire;
more earnest, more eager, with the languor in which
desire dies triumphant.

A less elaborate, less perverse kind of dancing is
to be seen in the cafés, in little pantomimic ballets,
imitated from French models, but done with a Spanish
simplicity of emphasis. There is, in such things, a
frank, devil-may-care indecency, part of a boisterous
hilarity, which has all the air of an accidental improvisation, as indeed it often is; and this hilarity is tossed
to and fro from stage to audience and from audience to
stage, as if a crowd of lively people had become a
little merry at the corner of a street. The Spanish
(look at their comic papers) are so explicit! It is
not cold, or calculated, like that other, more significant, kind of dancing; it is done with youth and
delighted energy, and as among friends, and by

people to whom a certain explicit kind of coarseness is natural.

V

Seville is not a religious city, as Valencia is; but it has woven the ceremonies of religion into its life, into its amusements, with a minuteness of adaptation certainly unparalleled. Nowhere as in Spain does one so realise the sacred drama of the Mass. The costumes, the processions, the dim lighting, the spectacular arrangement of the churches and ceremonies, the religious attitude of the people, kneeling on the bare stones, the penitent aspect of their black dresses and mantillas, intermingled with the bright peasant colours which seem to bring the poor people so intimately into association with the mysteries of religion : all this has its part in giving the Church its dramatic pre-eminence. And in Seville the ceremonies of the Church are carried out with more detail, more spectacular appeal, than anywhere else in Spain, that is to say, more than anywhere in the world. All Europe flocks to see the celebrations of Holy Week, which must have come down unchanged from the Middle Ages; a piece of immense mediæval childishness, which still suits the humour of Seville perfectly. And it is not only in Holy Week that one may see the most characteristic of all these ceremonies, the sacred dances in the Cathedral, but also at the great feast of the Immaculate Conception, which is peculiarly a Sevillan feast.

On that day, the 8th December, I attended Mass in the Cathedral. The gold and silver plate had been laid out by the side of the altar, crimson drapings covered the walls, the priests wore their " terno celeste," blue and gold vestments; the Seises, who were to dance later on, were there in their blue-and-white costume of the time of Philip III.; the acolytes wore gilt mitres, and carried silver-topped staves and blue canopies. There was a procession through the church, the Archbishop and the Alcaldia walking in state, to the sound of sad voices and hautboys, and amidst clouds of rolling white incense, and between rows of women dressed in black, with black mantillas over their heads. The Mass itself, with its elaborate ritual, was sung to the very Spanish music of Eslava: and the Dean's sermon, with its flowery eloquence, flowers out of the Apocalypse and out of the fields of " la Tierra de Maria Santísima," was not less typically Spanish. At five o'clock I returned to .the Cathedral to see the dance of the Seises. There was but little light except about the altar, which blazed with candles; suddenly a curtain was drawn aside, and the sixteen boys, in their blue and white costume, holding plumed hats in their hands, came forward and knelt before the altar. The priests, who had been chanting, came up from the choir, the boys rose, and formed in two eights, facing each other, in front of the altar, and the priests knelt in a semi-circle around them. Then an unseen orchestra began to play, and the boys put on their hats, and began to sing the *coplas* in honour of the Virgin :

> "O mi, O mi amada
> Immaculada ! "

as they sang, to a dance-measure. After they had sung the *coplas* they began to dance, still singing. It was a kind of solemn minuet, the feet never taken from the ground, a minuet of delicate stepping and intricate movement, in which a central square would form, divide, a whole line passing through the opposite line, the outer ends then repeating one another's movements while the others formed and divided again in the middle. The first movement was very slow, the second faster, ending with a pirouette; then came two movements without singing, but with the accompaniment of castanets, the first movement again very slow, the second a quick rattle of the castanets, like the rolling of kettle-drums, but done without raising the hands above the level of the elbows. Then the whole thing was repeated from the beginning, the boys flourished off their hats, dropped on their knees before the altar, and went quickly out. One or two verses were chanted, the Archbishop gave his bene-diction, and the ceremony was over.

And, yes, I found it perfectly dignified, perfectly religious, without a suspicion of levity or indecorum. This consecration of the dance, this turning of a

I

possible vice into a means of devotion, this bringing
of the people's art, the people's passion, which in
Seville is dancing, into the church, finding it a place
there, is precisely one of those acts of divine worldly
wisdom which the Church has so often practised in
her conquest of the world. And it is a quite logical
development of that very elaborate pantomime, using
the word in all seriousness, which the ceremonies of
the Church really are, since all have their symbolical
meaning, which they express by their gestures.
Already we find in them every art but one: poetry,
the very substance of the liturgy, oratory, music,
both of voices and instruments, sculpture, painting,
all the decorative arts, costume, perfume, every art
lending its service; and now at last dancing finds its
natural place there, in the one city of the world
where its presence is most perfectly in keeping.

Winter, 1898.

PRAGUE

PRAGUE

I

WOODED and watery Bohemia, though indeed no
longer on the sea-coast, might well have seemed to
Shakespeare, if he had really seen it, the place for a
tragical pastoral. Coming from Bayreuth to Prague,
one finds oneself, as soon as one has got well beyond
Karlsbad, in a totally new country. The very sky is
new, and I have seen an orange light of fire, break-
ing through barred clouds like a vision of the gate
of the Venusberg, which added a new experience to
my knowledge of sunsets. And the country is at
once wide-reaching and mountainous, rising into pine-
woods above quiet rivers, and widening out into green
and brown plains, hedgeless, with here and there a
corn-field, a flock of geese herded by a small boy, a
few goats, a few cows. All along the line, people
are bathing in the rivers, or lying with naked feet
among the grass. A boatman tows himself across,
reaching up to a rope above his head, as he stands
in his flat oblong boat, square at each end. The
scenery is wild and yet gentle, with many delicate
shades of green, fading into hills in which the mist
turns the pine-woods purple. And Prague itself,
seen from the Vyšehrad, once the acropolis of the

city, and now a melancholy waste of grass and crawling roads and modern fortifications, seems little more
than an accidental growth among green fields and
tree-covered hillsides, a wide land of woods and
meadows and streams. Seen from the Hradčin, the
Kremlin of Prague, it is a city of pointed spires, green
domes, and red, many-gabled roofs, through which
the Moldau wanders, carrying its five bridges ; and
it climbs the hill like Naples rising to Capodimonte.
All Prague is red and green, and part of its charm
for one, not only as one looks down upon it, seeing
the freshness of the green among the red, comes
from its homely, delightful way of filling up vacant
spaces with grass and trees, as in the vast Karlovo
Namĕsti, the only city square I know which is
almost a park, laid out with smooth grass and cool
trees and flower-beds planted in patterns, and yet an
actual city square, closed in by civic buildings, with
its fourteenth-century tower by the side of what was
once a Rathhaus out of whose windows Žižka had
flung councillors. And the green is everywhere,
spreading outward from the fortifications, high above
the city, where the children play on the grass, spots
of bright colour, and piling itself mountainously up
the Nebozizek, and softening the river with shadows,
and flowering out of the river in green islands.

The Moldau, which cuts Prague in two, is broad
and swift, golden under sunlight, as it hurries under
its five bridges, between the green banks and the
quay. Long rafts of floating timber, on which men

run to and fro with tall poles, pass slowly, hurrying
as they shoot the weir. Boats cross from side to
side, and one sees the slow, crossing gesture of men
with long-handled scoops, dredging in a barge. A
man stands on a heap of stones, in the very middle
of the weir, fishing. Half-naked figures, or figures
in bathing-gowns, move to and fro on the big brown
floating baths, or swing out on a trapeze over the
water. A sound of music comes from one of the
green islands, where people are sitting at café tables
under the trees. People drowse on the benches
by the side of the river.

Warm, full of repose, heavy with happy sleep, at
midday, at night the riverside becomes mysterious,
a romance. The water silvers; with its islands,
from which lights glimmer, it might be a lake, but
for the thunder of the weir, which comes to you as
you walk under the trees, or go out on a kind of
platform beside a dusty mill, from which you see
the water rushing violently towards the great wooden
stakes by the bridge. Lights move on the opposite
shore, at the foot of what seems a vast mountain,
dimly outlined. The bridge, at first invisible, a
detached line of lights, comes out gradually, as your
eyes accustom themselves to the night-mist, in the
palest of grey, like the ghost of a bridge. Beyond
and above, the Hradčin emerges in the same ghostly
outline, a long grey line against the sky, out of
which the cathedral spire points upward. It is a
view which seems to have been composed, almost

too full of the romantic elements to be quite natural; and it has something of whatever is strange, placid, and savage in the character of the Bohemians.

II

The real centre of Prague is the Karlův Most, or Karl Bridge, which crosses the Moldau on eight out of its sixteen arches. Begun in the fourteenth century, with its fifteenth-century tower and its mainly eighteenth-century statues, it may remind one at first sight of the Ponte Sant' Angelo at Rome ; but Bernini in his most fantastic mood never conceived anything so fantastic as these thirty stone and bronze figures of saints, martyrs, doctors of the Church, Our Saviour, and the suffering souls in purgatory. There is a crucifix erected with money mulcted from a Jew in 1606, in which the gilded bronze is washed and dusted and weather-stained into a ruddy and veined warmth. St John Nepomuc, the patron-saint of Prague, is in dark bronze, with the five stars around his halo, like five spikes of gold ; and near by is the marble slab marking the spot where he was flung over the bridge, a tiny bronze image representing him floating, with his crown of stars, down the river. For the most part, the saints are in rough-hewn stone, based at times with faintly outlined reliefs, bearing strange inscriptions, such as that which commemorates St John Nepomuc, who "conquered devils and turned 8000 Saracens and 2500 Jews to the Christian faith," the Jews and the Saracens being shown on their way to that pious moment. The strangest of all these monuments is a vast and rocky mass, surmounted by the figures of several saints, and opening in the midst to show three hollow and piteous figures in purgatory, lifting their chained hands towards the doorway, guarded on one side by a snarling dog, on the other by a gigantic Bohemian in uniform, with a fat stomach, endless moustaches, and a long sword hanging from his military cloak, as if to impress upon the minds of Bohemians that hell, for them at all events, was entirely Bohemian. There is a certain savagery in the whole aspect and record of this bridge, in its way of indicating the place where spiked heads rotted for ten years, the place where a just man was flung into the water by a tyrant, in the vindictive insistence on the fact that a reviling Jew's money had been taken to set up the crucifix. It is an always fierce and militant religion which has fixed these landmarks, a religion always armed against enemies, or suffering death at their hands. There is none of that rest which remains to the people of God in these large and active figures, who had laboured and suffered; as there is none of that rest which is beauty, here or elsewhere, in the endeavours after art of the Bohemians.

Visiting the older part of the Hradčin, one is impressed by an air of naked strength, of walls built only for defence, of a kind of contempt for decoration; everywhere is bare stone, hard wood; the Council Chamber has a brick floor, leather-covered tables, a wooden stool for the Archbishop, a dungeon-like room for the secretary. And in the Cathedral, the metropolitan church of St Vitus, the memorial statues are of men in armour, as if every one buried there had died by violence and in the act of fighting. In the barbaric Václavská Kaple, or Wenzel Chapel, the saint's helmet and coat of mail are preserved in a niche behind the altar. His statue, by Vischer of Nürnberg, stands in armour in a corner of this sombre place, where the faded frescoes are half outlined and half over-laid by smooth, unshaped masses of amethyst, chrysoprase, malachite, porphyry, set into the damp walls without pattern or design, blotching the rotting colours with crude heapings of precious stones. The Svato-Týnský-Chram, or Teyn Church, has also its men in armour carved upon stone tomb-stones; Tycho Brahe among them, holding his globe and compass, not far from the burial vault of the Wallensteins.

And in almost all its architecture Prague shows this over-emphatic, unæsthetic spirit. The Teyn Church, especially at night, rises with a really original romantic effect against the sky, out of the clustering roofs surrounding it; the Cathedral has its fine Gothic choir; here and there is a tower, impressive by its solidity. And it must be re-membered how much has been swept away in

fanatical wars; how little leisure for the cultivation of the arts has been left at any time to so
disturbed a people. But wherever you go in
Prague, you will find a bastard kind of architecture,
Renaissance crossed with Slavonic, which has little
sense of design and no sense of decoration, except
the overlaying of a·plain surface with protruding
figures. The Prašna Brana, or Powder Gate,
bristles with coats of arms, set there for historic,
not for artistic reasons, and roughly carved figures,
standing out from the surface of the walls without
symmetry or design; there are rococo palaces and
houses decorated with meaningless stucco ornament
and with monstrous caryatides supporting nothing,
vast griffins or heraldic eagles, like excrescences
upon the rock; over one doorway is the legend
of St Julian, with the miraculous stag; at street
corners, in little niches, are painted Christs, dripping
with blood, like the horrible seated figure in the
Teyn Church. And the taste of the people runs all
to angles. Every square is surrounded by lines of
houses of irregular height, set irregularly; when a
square is sub-divided, it is inset with a triangle;
every corner is turned so as to make as many angles
as possible. The pavement is mosaicked into squares
and triangles, and these angles are carried into the
sky. Spires bristle up from every church, and at
the corners of every tower, and these spires, pointed,
wedge-shaped, with an occasional bulbous dome,
like the domes of Moscow, are set with a family of

little spires growing out of them at alternate angles. They are seen, a mere suggestion, on the twelfth-century church of St George, in the Hradčin; gradually the cluster of spires develops, century by century, until we come to the fifteenth-century west façade of the Teyn Church and the corner towers of the Powder Gate. This detail, the only invention in architecture of the Bohemians, is typical of the people, so alive to the utility of straight lines, the emphasis of sharp angles, so insensitive to the gradual beauty of the curve, the more delicate harmonies of proportion. There is something, in their way of building, fierce, violent, unrestrained, like the savagery of their fighting, of their fighting songs, of their fighting music. "All ye warriors of God," says the Taborite war-song of Žižka, "strike and kill, spare none!" "Woe to you, Huss!" retorts a Catholic song. And nothing is more curious than to contrast this fiery spirit, showing itself in energy of line and angularity of outline, with the gentleness, the soft colour, the placidity of the wide green spaces within the city, and the vast green plains and hillsides in whose midst the city has entrenched itself.

III

The Bohemians have produced nothing beautiful in any of the plastic arts; but in literature, for the most part given up to histories of piety and savagery, they have produced one book of genius, in whose hardness, quaintness, crudity, and vigorous, unbeautiful detail, I find all the characteristic qualities of the race, illuminated, here only, by that light which is imagination. The full title of the book is: "The Labyrinth of the World and the Paradise of the Heart; that is, a book that clearly shows that this world and all matters concerning it are nothing but confusion and giddiness, pain and toil, deceit and falsehood, misery and anxiety, and lastly, disgust of all things and despair; but he who remains in his own dwelling within his heart, opening it to the Lord God alone, will obtain true and full peace of mind and joy." It was written in 1623, at the age of thirty-one, by John Amos Komensky, better known as Comenius, who, later in life, wrote largely on education, and has been remembered, outside his own country, as an educational authority, and no more. But Komensky was something more than this, and his one imaginative work, written, as the title indicates, from a religious conviction (he was a pastor of the "Bohemian Brethren"), is a kind of "Pilgrim's Progress," with something of "Gulliver's Travels" in it as well, and it may be compared, as a piece of literature, with both these "criticisms of life." It was written almost at the same time as the "Pilgrim's Progress," and Count Lützow, who has translated it into English with great skill and accuracy, has shown good judgment

in rendering it into an English for the most part as
homely as Bunyan's.

Like Rabelais, but with less intentional extravagance, Komensky will use ten synonyms for one
statement; he writes all in verbs and nouns, which
hammer on our ears with the clatter of the fighting
peasants' flails. "When I inclined my ears, everything was full of knocking, stamping, scrubbing,
whispering and screaming," he tells us, in his first
impression of the world; and, of the ignorant
physicians: "Then they immediately cooked, stewed,
roasted, broiled, cauterised, cooled, burnt, hacked,
sawed, pricked, sewed together, bound up, greased,
hardened, softened, wrapped up, poured out
medicines." He calls mean things by their names,
and catches at whatever words will render his
meaning most nakedly. He writes in squares and
chequers, in a style like the pavement of Prague.
But, in him, the stern Bohemian piety turns to a
strange kind of spiritual insight, for which it is his
genius to have found an appropriate form.

Komensky's mind was a kind of mechanical intelligence, moving with hard precision, allegorising by
rule, with a shrewdness a little sharpened by a kind
of abstract malice. He builds up his allegory by a
process of reasoning, coming after the poets and
makers of metaphors, and using for his own purpose
what remains over when the poetry has cooled.
Poetry may often be truth concentrated into a metaphor; Komensky takes hold of the metaphor, and

resolves it to its original essence of truth; as when he sees Death shooting arrows, and, looking closer, perceives that Death has nothing but a bow, and that each man fashions his own arrow. Here, as always, imagination comes to him through logic, through a literal, matter-of-fact unravelling of ideas or figures, taken at their word. When he first considers the vanity of the world's works, this is how he sees it: "Some, indeed, collected sweepings and divided them amongst themselves; some hurried here and there with timber and stones, or dragged them up with a windlass, and then dropped them; some dug up earth, and conveyed it from place to place; the others occupied themselves with little bells, looking-glasses, alembics, rattles, and other playthings; others also played with their own shadow, measuring and pursuing it and catching at it; and all this so vigorously that many groaned and sweated, and some, indeed, also injured themselves." It is like one watching the swarming of insects, mocking their labours by the mere enumeration of them, emptying his human contempt on them for busying themselves with ends not his own, measuring their doings by the standard of his own mind. There is a fine intellectual callousness in it, a cold cruelty of logic which is almost a more fundamental criticism of life than Swift's lacerating satire. One sees that Swift is in a rage, and one allows for the exaggeration and partiality of one who is in a rage. But Komensky is neither in a rage nor does he seem to

be touched with pity, nor yet to laugh at the follies
which he sees.   He is as chilled as Plotinus on his
stone; he seems to be but a vast pair of eyes and
ears, sucking in appearances, and transmuting them
coldly into observations.   The irony, and the con-
demning force of the truth, come in as if by accident;
the philosophy lies all in the framework, like a rigid
thing of mere hard measurement.

The lesson which Komensky has for us, the
lesson of all disinterested searchers in the world, is
this: "I have seen and beheld and understood that
I myself am nothing, understand nothing, possess
nothing; neither do others; it is but a vain con-
ceit."   On the way he has seen Fame: "It befell
that one arrived claiming immortality, who, asked
what deed worthy of immortal memory he had done,
replied that he had destroyed the most glorious
thing in the world of which he knew."   He has
seen the great of the earth, seated on high and
toppling seats, on the very edge of a great height,
where they might be seen by all who are below:
"the higher a seat was, the easier it was to shake
it."   The rich sit chained in darkness, counting and
kissing the links of their chains, which they think
to be of pure gold.   Lovers stand in front of a gate
called betrothment : "In front of it there was a wide
square in which crowds of people of both sexes
walked about, and each one looked into the eyes of
the other; and not only this, but they also looked
at one another's ears, nose, teeth, neck, tongue,

hands, feet, and other limbs; also did each measure the other—how tall, how broad, how stout, or how slender he was." The newsmen blow their whistles in the street, and men rejoice or lament according to the cheerful or mournful sound of the whistle. The rhetoricians keep school: "where, behold, many stood holding brushes, and they discussed as to how words either written or spoken into the air could be coloured green, red, black, white, or whatever colour a man might wish." The poets are seen to be "a troup of agile young men who were weighing syllables on balancès, and measuring them by the span, rejoicing meanwhile, and skipping round them." The natural philosophers are trying to crack the nuts of the tree of nature: "some, indeed, stared till their eyes pained them, and gnawed till they broke their teeth." The pilgrim inquires after the men of learning, and finds them fighting with "reeds and quills, which they loaded with powder that had been dissolved in water"; unlike other fighters, these do not even spare the dead, but still hack at their bodies. The books, out of which they get their learning, are found to be so many gallipots in a chemist's shop, containing "remedies against the ailments of the mind," which the most part cram until they are sick. Merchants trading by land and by sea are seen at their hard and perilous business; and it is in the description of a storm at sea that we find the most vivid and sustained piece of writing in the book.

K

"The Labyrinth of the World" ends with a cry of despair: "O God, God, God! God, if thou art a God, have mercy on wretched me!" But Komensky•has not finished; we turn the page and are in "The Paradise of the Heart." The satirist, the observer, the contemner of worldly things, has given place to the Christian, the mystic, the Quietist. A voice is heard saying: "Return! return whence thou camest to the house of the heart, and then close the doors behind thee." A little light comes in through the cracked and dusty windows, and then brighter and brighter light, and a transforming energy which cleanses everything in the house, and presently the presence of God himself, as guest and then as bridegroom, and an inner illumination in which all that has been seen awry is seen in its true order. The pilgrim learns how he may live in the world without living as the world lives, realising now "that the world is not so heavy that it may not be endured, nor so valuable that its loss need be regretted."

IV

There is one corner of Prague which has kept more than any other its mediæval aspect, combining in itself many of the contrasts of this contradictory city; the Jewish quarter, which lies between the Staroměstké Náměsti and the river. The synagogue, built in the twelfth century, outside like a monstrous

dwelling, inside like a dungeon, made in the image
of a wizard's cell, with its low roof and heavy walls
black with age, pierced with narrow windows, its
railed-off space in the centre, in which a . chair and
desk seem to await a scribe, its narrow seats, each
with its little desk, its tall candelabras and mean
candlesticks, in some of which a candle is guttering
out, its banner of the time of Ferdinand III., its
suspended cloth or robe, hung with bells like the
robe of the High Priest, its strange ornaments of
wood and copper, as of some idolatry to which
graven images had never lent grace, concentrates
in itself all the horror of the Ghetto. And the
Ghetto swarms about it in a medley of narrow
streets and broad empty spaces, a pestilent circle
of evil smells and half-naked children, and slatternly
Jews and Jewesses, in the midst of shops of old
boots and old clothes, and old houses with coats
of arms over their doors and broken ornaments on
their walls. Out of the midst of this confusion a
short street leads to the old burial-ground, hidden
behind its high, enclosing wall. This graveyard
in the midst of the city, in which no graves have
been dug for more than a hundred years, carries
back the mind, as one walks among its alleys and
garden-plots of tombs, to an unknown antiquity.
The tombstones are crowded and pressed together,
rows of them overlap the same grave, and they
huddle together, in a forced companionship, leaning
this way and that, battered and chipped, with worn

lettering and broken ornaments. Most have inscriptions in Hebrew, with symbolical records of
tribe or name, a fish for Fischer, a stag for Hirsch,
two hands for the tribe of Aaron. Some are family
tombs, in which the broken lid of a sarcophagus
shows a glimpse of bones among the casual heapings
of time. Some are famous tombs, such as that of
Rabbi Loewe, the friend of Tycho Brahe, a tall
slab, crowned with a cone, and still heaped with
little stones on every ledge, after the Jewish fashion
of commemorating the dead. But now all cling
together in a sad equality. The trees have grown
familiar with the tombs, turning grey and green
together, as they share the same weather, age after
age. One tree has bent over and riveted itself
upon the edge of a gravestone, which it presses
down into the earth under its weight. The alders
are shrivelled and twisted, with but little foliage,
as they cover the tombs with a hand's-breadth of
melancholy shade. The lichen creeps up their
trunks, which are cracked and dry. Weeds and
thorns grow about their roots, the grass is everywhere, with bare patches here and there of black
earth, close about the tombstones.

The sky was turning towards sunset as I wandered
about the alleys under the trees, and the last pale
rays of the sun filtered through the leaves and
gave a sadder light to the broken edges of grey
stone. Now and then a blackbird crossed between
the tombs and the sunlight. Towards the farther

end, where the graves are fewer and the trees grow more freely, children were playing on the grass. It seemed to me as if one were seeing all the graves of all the people who had ever died. These tombs, as no others had ever done, seemed to sum up the real meaning of our memory of the dead, the real way in which they crowd together, dwindling miserably, as time carries them further and further away from the general memory. They were inexpressibly human, these poor gravestones, on so few of which had any people now living come to put the pious stones of remembrance.

V

Prague in summer has the aspect of a Southern, rather than of a Northern city, for the people are out of doors all day long, walking in the streets for the mere pleasure of walking in them, and sitting under the trees on the islands in the river and in the gardens of many cafés and in the parks which lead into the country in every direction. They bring their books and their work with them, they bring little paper packets of sweets, and there is generally a band playing as they sit at tables drinking their "white coffee" or their beer. Bohemian music has a kind of fiery monotony, its polka beat marked with all the emphasis of ceaseless cymbals, in an orchestra arranged after a somewhat savage fashion of its own. Popular music, and the characteristically Bohemian music of Dvořák and Smetana, has a singular mixture of barbarism, of something windy and savage, and of a kind of conventionality. There is no passion in it, but a sort of primitive folk-rhythm, full of surprises to the Western ear, with sudden spirals of the flutes and hautboys, leaps and clashes of the cymbals, enveloping outbursts of the brass. The people are for the most part quiet and good-humoured people, in whom it is curious to trace the mixture of Slavonic and German blood. The pure German type, which begins to lessen at Karlsbad, is hardly to be seen at Prague; the faces are more nervous, with sharper eyes, the figures are slimmer, less shapeless. They are often very blonde, at times very dark, and there is something a little wild, even in the soft beauty of blonde women, a fiery sweetness, a certain strangeness as of unfamiliar lights amid the shadows of still water; a little of the soft, unconscious savagery of the animals man has tamed, but which have never quite forgotten the forest. But they are not perilous, like the Hungarians; sly, sometimes, but simple. Children and young girls are often delicious, with their white skin and pale gold hair, which in some lights takes a faint shade of green, like the hair of a certain portrait by Palma Vecchio, known as the portrait of his daughter, in the gallery at Vienna. The children of poor people go bare-footed, sometimes the women; in the country,

women and children alike, a habit which is but one
among many likenesses to the habits of the Irish
peasant. Sometimes, under the invariable handkerchief which they wear about their heads, one sees
flat, broad faces which suggest the Calmuck; like
all women who do the work of men in the open
air, they are old women at twenty. And the
poorer people are for the most part a little
slatternly, without natural taste in dressing; true
peasants, peasants of the North, who have none
of the elegance of the Southern peasant. And
all these people have, in their faces, in their de-
meanour, something of the seriousness of people
in Protestant countries; Catholics as they have
been for three hundred years, they seem to have
not yet outlived the Protestant temperament; seem
still, and only not through an accident in images
which has really happened, to be honouring Huss
when they worship St John Nepomuc.

VI

Prague is a city of contrasts, and it is not to be
understood until one has seen the Příkopy as well as
the Hradčin, the modern Václavské Náměsti, as well
as the ancient arcades about the Staroměstké
Náměsti, and has realised that all these contrasts are
so many parts of a single national life, and that they
are, after all, only the more visible half of that

"slata Praha," that "golden Prague," which the
Bohemian sees, not only with his eyes, but with his
memory. The older parts of the town give one a
strange sensation of being still in the Middle Ages,
and they are sombre, at moments menacing, as one
comes upon great archways leading into narrow
alleys, or opening into vaulted inner rooms, or great
courtyards. Twisting lanes lead from street to
street, restaurants or cafés show a glimmering light
at the end of a long passage plunged in darkness;
wherever one passes one gets fantastic glimpses
under arcades and archways, people moving across
roughly paved squares, by a flickering light, or
turning down a narrow passage under a low doorway. There is a modern Prague which is growing
up in the image of Vienna, with tall characterless
houses, and modish shops, and it is indeed to be
feared that this new Prague will gradually over-
grow all that is left of the old city. But at
present the contrast can still be enjoyed without
more than an agreeable sense of incongruity, as
one passes, at the turn of a street, from the somewhat melancholy slumber of an old palace, into an
atmosphere of life and bustle, as of a contented
town-life going steadily on.

And this life of to-day, which has at last become
national, passionately national, so that the names of
the streets are no longer to be seen in German, and
the Čech theatre would hesitate to perform an opera
of Wagner, because he was a German, and riots can

break out in a German theatre, and actresses be
fought over in the streets because they act in
German; this new outbreak of national life is fed
upon memories. The Bohemian still sees a phantom
city, behind this city in which electric trams take
him to the foot of the Vyšehrad, a city more real to
him than even what remains of his national monuments. His memory is a memory of martyrs, of
executions, of the savageries of religion and of
political conflict, Catholics against Protestants,
Germans against Čechs; he remembers, as he passes
the place where the Bethelem Chapel of Huss once
stood, the burning of Huss at Constance; he remembers the flails and pitchforks of Žižka, he
remembers Wallenstein, Radetzky. Here, outside
the Rathhaus, were the executions of the 21st June,
1621, after the battle of the White Mountain, in
which Protestantism died. Here, on the Staroměstká
Věž, the tower which he passes under when he
crosses the river, the twenty-seven heads were left
rotting for ten years. He is not taken over the
castle without being shown the window from which
the three councillors were flung in 1618, an act of
" defenestration," as it has been called by Count
Lützow, the historian of Bohemia, which brought
about the Thirty Years' War. War after war has
devastated Prague, spoiling it of much that was
finest and most characteristic in its buildings; but to
the Bohemian no stone that has been violently cast
down is forgotten. Prague is still the epitome of

the history of his country; he sees it as a man sees the woman whom he loves, with her first beauty, and he loves it as a man loves a woman, more for what she has suffered.

SUMMER, 1897 and 1899.

MOSCOW

Moscow.
From a print in the British Museum

MOSCOW

I

THE road to Moscow, if you enter Russia at the
Polish frontier, lies for nearly a thousand miles
through the midst of a great desert, which has at
once the vast, level extent and the delicately
changing colour of the sea; with a sense of loneliness almost as absolute as that of the sea, to the
voyager in a ship. Resembling, at moments, the
Roman Campagna, these steppes have their own
very personal kind of beauty, in which the monotony
of their apparent endlessness is after all only that
monotony which is an element of all fine style,
in nature as well as in art. Looking out of the
windows of the train, as it goes slowly on, day
and night, you see on both sides an interminable
plain of short grass, unbroken by hedges; at
intervals a forest, a plantation, or a few pines or
birches; here and there a little wooden hut in the
midst of a pine-wood, like the cabin of some Thoreau;
here and there a thatched village, with sunflowers
before its doors, or a small town, with blue and gold
domes; and, between house and house, profound
loneliness, not a human being, not an animal, not
a breath of smoke, visible. Everywhere the land-

scape makes pictures, but not in the manner of most
landscapes; delicate pictures, full of rest, and of still
trees, with perhaps a single human figure, faintly
indicated, such as Corot painted; with something
of his favourite colouring, something also of his
charm of composition, for once absolutely natural in
nature.   Where, at times, a cornfield would rise up,
brown and gold, out of the green plain, a few men
and women reaping, it was with a noble gesture,
reminding one of attitude as it is refined and preserved
for us in pictures, that a woman, perhaps, would
pause, the sickle curved for a moment above her
head.   Finely monotonous, sensitive, full of subdued
colour, with all the charm of natural refinement
in what is for the most part uncultivated, unspoilt,
not yet turned to useful ends by the impatient
absorption of civilisation, this sea of land, flowing
gradually up to the vague outskirts of Moscow,
prepared me, in my slow journey through it, for a
not too sudden entrance upon the bewilderments of
the city.

Of Moscow itself not much was visible from the
train, and I went, like all the world, to that
traditional enimence, Vorobievy Gory, the Sparrow
Hills, where the terrace of a restaurant marks the
place from which Napoleon and his army came suddenly within sight of Moscow.   Seen at sunset,
across deep woods and wide green fields, through
which the Moskva curved gently, as if embracing it,
the city seemed to lie stretched at full length.   A

trail of black smoke from a factory, and a column of
brownish smoke going up from a fire, darkened a
space of clear sky above the glittering of innumerable
white spires and turrets, which shone with a brightness far beyond that of the golden and many-
coloured domes which glowed between them.   The
twisted lines of the Kremlin stood out sharply above
their battlements, the white outer wall seeming to
rise out of the river; beyond, pinnacled roofs
wandered indefinitely, their colours, and the colours
of many walls, repeating the exact greens of the
fields which lay about them, as if a fierce sun had
flashed up an actual reflection upon them. Gradually
the light faded out, until the city looked like a long,
dim, thin line, ridging the plain.   Coming back in
the dark, on the little steamer, to drift over those
bright, visibly rippling waters, between the lights
and deep wooded shadows of the banks, was at one
moment almost like being on the Venetian lagoons,
at another, like being on an Irish lake.   Just before
landing, as we came into the midst of the city, I saw
the modern, not very interesting Church of the
Saviour for once effective, rising hugely into the sky,
as if carved solidly out of grey cloud.

II

Charming, for all its strangeness, when seen at
night, or from a distance, Moscow is without charm,

in spite of its strangeness, when seen clearly and by
day. Built, like Rome, on seven hills, it radiates
outwards, circle beyond circle, from the central
height of the Kremlin; the old, or "Chinese town,"
heaped within its white wall, cut off sharply from
the "white town" of shops and public buildings and
large houses, which dwindles into the first ring of
dusty boulevards; and from this the "earthen
town" stretches to the outer ring of boulevards;
and then the suburbs begin, vague, interminable,
and seeming, long before they have reached the
ramparts which close in the thirty-six miles of the
city's circumference, to have passed into the open
country. Like everything in Russia, it is by its size
that it first impresses you. Vast, vaguely defined, so
casual in its division of time, of day and night, of
the hours in the day, full of heavy leisure, unoccupied space, this city, next to the largest city in
Europe, has much of the aspect of some extraordinary
village, which has sprung up, and widened gradually,
about a citadel. Its seven hills have done something
to leave more than usual of the open air about it, in
wide, windless spaces, brooded over by the wings of
innumerable pigeons. Everywhere are vast, unpaved
squares, surrounded by a rope of twisted wire,
stretched from post to post, or by temporary
wooden railings, propped up at vague intervals.
Cross the river by the bridge which lies between
the Kremlin and the church of the Saviour, and you
will see, between weir and weir, ducks floating on

the water, a ferry-boat waiting to take people over,
red figures paddling by the banks, or wading across
with tucked up trousers or petticoats; clothes being
beaten on a row of planks which stretch from the
dusty shore to the queer little sailing boats moored
in mid-stream.   Everywhere you will find village
scenes, the trees and water and width, the fields
even, of the real country.   And the life of the
people, the arrangement of the houses, have the
characteristics of village life: these houses, often
only one storey high, rarely higher than two storeys,
built often of wood, like log-huts, and with a
wooden palisade in front of their strip of garden, or
wide, dusty court, in which one hears the flutter of
fowls and the gabble of white turkeys.   Outside,
on the irregular pavement, village carts jolt by, an
unending procession, with a sound like the sound of
an army marching; the cabs, labouring slowly at
full speed, are like the primitive vehicles of old-
fashioned folk in the country.   The markets, which
on so many days of the week cover with stalls, and
stacked carts, and heaped baskets, the vacant squares
and open spaces of boulevards, are like village
markets; and the people themselves, with their red
shirts and top-boots, have the air of people who till
the soil.

But of the repose, the freshness, which we
associate with life in villages, there is nothing.
Deafening in summer, with its streets and squares
paved irregularly with cobbles, and surging up

and down in waves and hollows, over which the wheels go rocking and clattering all day long; silent in winter, when the sledges glide over the white and even snow; there is always the oppression of noise or of silence, some not quite natural suspense of nature. At Moscow everything is in extremes; the weather halves the year between the two burdens of sun and ice, and the whole aspect of the city is one of preparation for those extremes. The iron-bound pavements slope down gradually to the street, in order to assist the toiler through snow in passing from one level to another; gutters run across the pavement at every water-pipe to make natural channels for the water; the costume, even in summer, of the *likhatchi* drivers is an immense padded overcoat, falling like a petticoat to the feet, and swathing the body as if it enclosed a Falstaff; the top-boots, worn even in summer by three-fourths of the population, suggest the heavy walking of the winter. And in nothing are these extremes more emphatic than in the colours which clash against each other everywhere in the streets, colours which absorb and fatigue the eye, leaving it without a cool shadow to rest upon.

In Russia everything is large and everything is loud. In the vast village of Moscow the buildings are all built broad, not high, because there is so much space to cover. The public squares, unpaved and surrounded by a little rim of cobbles, are as big as meadows. The arcades and passages, with their cellars below, their shops above, their glass roofs, are so enormous that they could hold the Passage des Panoramas, and the Burlington Arcade, and the galleries at Milan, without filling more than a corner of them. Colours shriek and flame; the Muscovite eye sees only by emphasis and by contrast; red is completed either by another red or by a bright blue. There are no shades, no reticences, no modulations. The restaurants are filled with the din of vast mechanical organs, with drums and cymbals; a great bell clashes against a chain on all the trams, to clear the road; the music which one hears is a ferocity of brass. The masons who build the houses build in top-boots, red shirts, and pink trousers; the houses are painted red or green or blue; the churches are like the temples of savage idols, tortured into every unnatural shape and coloured every glaring colour. Bare feet, osier-sandals, and legs swathed in rags, pass to and fro among the top-boots of the middle classes, the patent leather boots of the upper classes, like the inner savagery of a race still so near barbarism, made evident in that survival of the foot-gear of primitive races.

Nothing in Moscow is quite like anything one has seen anywhere else; and no two houses, all of which are so unlike the houses in any other country, are quite like one another. Their roofs are almost invariably painted green, and the water-pipes make a sort of green edging round the house-front. But the colours of the houses are endless : green, pink, blue, brown, red, chocolate, lilac, black even, rarely two of the same colour side by side, and rarely two of so much as the same general shape. Every shop has its walls painted over with rude pictures of the goods to be found inside; the draper has his row of clothed dummies, the hatter his pyramid of hats, the greengrocer his vegetables, the wine-seller his many-coloured bottles. Fruit-stalls meet one everywhere, and from the flower-like bouquet of fruits under their cool awnings there is a constant, shifting glow, the yellows and reds of apples, the purple of plums, the green and yellow of melons, and the crisp, black-spotted pink of melons sliced. And in these coloured streets, which in summer flame with the dry heat of a furnace, walk a multitude of coloured figures, brighter than the peasants of a comic opera; and the colours of their shirts and petticoats and handkerchiefs and bodices flame against the sunlight.

III

Set in such a frame, itself at all points so strange in shape and colour, the Kremlin and the churches, with their glittering domes, on which the symbolical Russian cross has made a footstool of the crescent, are but the last in a series of shocks with which this inexhaustible city greets one. All Moscow is distorted by eccentricity ; the hand of a madman is visibly upon it. Not only the unfortunate architect, but, I doubt not, the incalculable brain of Ivan the Terrible, gave its insane discordancy to the church of Vassily Blajenny; and that church, with its vegetable nightmare, its frantic falseness, its rapt disequilibrium, as of a dancing dervish whirled at last into fixity, is but the extreme symbol of all that attempts to be elaborate or ornate in Moscow. The Kremlin is like the evocation of an Arabian sorcerer, called up out of the mists and snows of the North; and the bells hung in these pagan, pagoda-like belfries seem to swing there in a last paradox, as if to drive away the very demons that have fixed them in mid-air. The church of Vassily Blajenny, in which few styles of architecture are not seen in some calculated or unconscious parody, is like the work of a child playing with coloured squares and cubes and triangles; its originality is that of a caricature; nowhere does it approach beauty, except in the corner porches to the doors, and in a certain conventional pattern, Turkish in design, which runs round a portion of the base. False windows are set to break the order of any surface left plain; not a line is allowed to flow, but every line must be tortured, broken as if on the wheel. The domes, of copper and painted lead and three-cornered tiles, are made to suggest the distortion of natural, growing things, pine-apples, pears, lemons, artichokes; they bristle with knobs, they bulge into excrescences; twisting upwards into a knot, for the most part in coils of alternate colours. The whole structure is a series of additions, and every addition is a fresh start, carried out without relation to any other portion; with an actual care, indeed, that there may be no repetition, no balance, of window or gable or dome or platform or turret. Within, there is a like confusion of little chapels, eleven in number, their walls cut into brief lengths, set at odd angles, painted in bright gold, and covered with the pictures of saints; a narrow passage, like the secret passage in a Gothic castle, leads from chapel to chapel, running round the outer edge of the building; so narrow that you can only just walk in it, so low that the roof is almost upon your head; and these walls are painted in heavy lines and patterns of green and red, with squares and knobs roughening the surface. The chapels, you would think, were themselves low, till, looking up, you see a shaft rising to a great height, from which a large painted face, seeming to lean over from the midst of the dome, looks down at you with outspread hands.

Russian architecture, the architecture which has set up for the worship of God these monstrous shrines, which might seem to have been built for Vishnu and Krishna, has its origin, certainly, in the East; but it has preserved only the eccentricity of the East, without its symmetry, its obedience to its own laws. The art of the East is like Eastern music, obeying laws to which our eyes and our ears have no response. But it has its origin in real nature closely observed and deliberately conventionalised; while Russian architecture, which seems to proceed from an imaginary assumption to an impossible conclusion, has no standard of beauty to which its caprices of line can appeal, but presents itself rather as a wildly inhuman grotesque, without root in nature or limitation in art. All the violence of the yellow, Mongolian East is in these temples, which break out into bulbs, and flower into gigantic fruits and vegetables of copper and tiles and carved stone; which are full of crawling and wriggling lines, of a kind of cruelty in form; in which the gold of the sun, the green of the earth's grass, and a blue which is to the blue of the sky what hell is to heaven, mock and deform the visible world in a kind of infernal parody. When, even, these lines run into finer shapes, and these colours melt into more delicate harmonies, they are still too full of mere curiosity, too odd, to be really beautiful. Ornament is heaped up with the profusion of the barbarian, to whom wealth means display; colour must decorate colour in one unending series, as sauce sharpens sauce in Russian cookery; line must envelop line until arabesque has become entanglement; height and breadth must alike extend themselves, for their own sake, and not for the emphasis which they may give, the elaboration they may permit, to a great central idea. Structure is but

a series of accretions, whose aim is to be unexpected.

Yet, abandoning oneself to their fantasy, what
pictures these domed and turreted walls, these
zigzags of sharp colour, make against the sky,
glowing with heat, dashing off the rays of the sun
as from many shields and helmets, coming up like
strange growths from among the trees, pointing into
the sky with lifted hands and outspread fingers!
There are certain old Burmese-looking towers on
the walls of the Kremlin where the green of the
spires is made by an incrustation of small green tiles,
shaped like leaves, and with slightly crinkled edges:
one might fancy almost an actual coating of leaves.
The crenellated outer walls of the Kremlin, with
their winglike and open battlements, with just room
enough to fall through in the space between wing
and wing, might hold all the Arabian Nights in their
midst; and their many gates, which might have
been built by Crusaders who had come from among
the Saracens, seem to await strange pilgrims, who
have crossed the green desert in cavalcades, with
their horses and mules laden with treasures.
Moscow, indeed, seems to have been consciously
arranged for atmospheric effects by some cunning
artist in stage scenery. Against certain dull skies,
seen even in summer, the gaudy blue of domes
softens to a real fineness of tint; and how effectively
that blue must be set off by the leaden skies of
winter, thick with snow! From the Krasnaïa Square

at night the little dingy row of trees settles like
hanging foliage upon the red wall of the Kremlin,
draping its unshaded brightness with a veil of
delicate green.   Green roofs and walls, against the
soft green sky which sometimes hangs over Moscow
after sunset, harmonise daintily ;   and on certain
late afternoons I have admired the new, lowered
colour of white towers, turret above turret, their
angles outlined with green, which in that light looks
like green moss on an old ruin, or upon actual
crumbling rock.

IV

The worship of painted images, on which so much
emphasis is laid by the Russian Church, has led, in
the adornment of their churches, to a heightening
of that natural Russian tendency to add detail to
detail, without assimilation, and without spacing.
The older churches are filled with paintings of
saints, and Scriptural and legendary scenes, set side
by side with no more than a thin gold frame between
them;   all on gold backgrounds, all in missal
painters' colours;   most in the same traditional
enlargement of life-size, and with the same vague
sense of reality.   They have nothing of the fine,
primitive angularity of Byzantine work, which they
seem to imitate ;   they are at once cold and in-
correct ;   without either scattering or convergence of
colour, wholly without design ;   and they fill every

inch of wall, and every corner and circle of the
ceiling, climbing up into the domes out of the cellar-
like narrowness of small chapels. About this
childish plastering of pictures upon the walls, a
multitude of gilded pillars, shrines, tombs, relics,
banners, slabs, balustrades, and the glittering doors
of the iconostase itself, build up a house of gold,
which weighs upon one like a burden. The priests,
with their long hair and Christ-like presence,
wearing heavy vestments of blue and red velvet
and gold-embroidered stuff (in which one sees the
hieratic significance of the blue of the domes) pass
through the concealing door from the presence of
the people to the presence of God, the door which,
at the most sacred moment, shuts them in upon that
presence ; and a choir of sad, deep Russian voices,
the voices of young men, chants antiphonally and in
chorus, weaving, in a sort of instrumental piece in
which the voices are the instruments, a heavy veil
of music, which trembles like a curtain before the
shrine.

And it is in another house of gold, heaped with
all the coloured things of the world, that the Russian
has set his earthly rulers. The Palace of the
Kremlin is the most sumptuous, the most spacious,
of royal palaces ; and its Treasury is one vast,
visible symbol of all that is barbaric and conquering
in the power of Russia. Thrones and dominions,
principalities and powers, all the nations of the
earth are seen bringing tribute, and their tribute

is heaped there like the spoils of a victorious army. Here are crowns, globes, sceptres, constellated with jewels, which flash fire from one to another as the light outlines their fantastic and elaborate patterns : the crown of Siberia, the crown of Kazan, the crown of Astrakhan. Here is the carved ivory throne of the last Emperor of Constantinople ; the throne of Boris Godounov, the gift of a Shah of Persia, in which every inch of framework is covered with slabs of solid gold, and the gold is thickly inlaid with turquoises and garnets, pearls and rubies ; the throne of Ivan the Terrible, the gift of another Shah of Persia, incrusted with 9000 precious stones, bordered with turquoises, framed on front and sides with worked silver, on which elephants walk and hares run, in the midst of silver meadows and forests, wrought so delicately that they seem to be embroidered. It is the East which one sees heaped here, in this orgy of jewels and gold, heaped like toys of which children do not know the value. It is the East in tribute, becoming the master of those who have come near enough to take its treasures ; and one sees Russia taking them barbarously, greedy of coloured baubles, insatiable, gorging itself with pomp and brilliance, which the wiser Persians had known how to subordinate, composing them into harmonies of their own.

And, in the very heart of this royal palace, after you have passed through its vast azure and gold spaces, in which the pomp of to-day can be so effective, you find also that cruelty, insanity, distortion, which flaunt themselves in the church of Vassily Blajenny. In the Terem, the seventeenth-century belvedere, with its five storeys built one out of another, the roofs are low, the ceilings vaulted and squared into odd angles; walls and ceilings are painted in red, blue, green, and gold, and a network of broad lines, twisted into all kinds of arabesques, coils about doors and walls and corners, and swarms across the ceilings; not an inch of surface is left plain, colour seems to be embroidered upon colour, all is ornament, and bright ornament, like the web of an Eastern carpet; the barred windows are of painted glass, and the sunlight sets their colours moving on the floor like living patterns. Little low room opens out of little low room, the red out of the blue, and the green out of the red; here, under an obscure ceiling of painted saints, the patriarchs have assembled; here, generations of emperors have slept. To be in one of these hot and many-coloured rooms is like being shut into the heart of a great tulip. Only fantastic and barbarous thoughts could reign here; life lived here could but be unreal, as if all the cobwebs of one's brain had externalised themselves, arching overhead and draping the four walls with a tissue of such stuff as dreams are made of. And it could easily seem as if unhuman faces grinned from among the iron trellis of doors, as if ropes and chains twisted themselves about doorways and ceilings, as if the floor crawled with strange scales, and the windows broke into living flames, and every wall burned inwards. The brain, driven in upon itself from such sombre bewilderments imprisoning it, could but find itself at home in some kind of tyrannical folly, perhaps in actual madness.

V

To live in Moscow is to undergo the most interesting, the most absorbing fatigue, without escape from the ceaseless energy of colour, the ceaseless appeal of novelty. Mere existence there is a constant strain on the attention, in which shock after shock bewilders the eyes, hurrying the mind from point to point of restless wonder, of unsatisfying admiration. To the dweller in Western cities, where an old, slow civilisation has had time to cover many stones with moss, bringing leisure into men's minds, and the quiet of ancient things about their houses, Moscow has all the barbarism of a civilisation which is but two centuries old. It is a barbarism, certainly, that has seized many of the delightful things which other nations have left for its fresh instinct to lay a new value upon. The Russians have all the luxuries of civilised barbarians; their cookery and their baths are the most elaborate in the world. The saying that Russia is rotten before it is ripe has but little

significance at Moscow, though its meaning may
perhaps be divined at St Petersburg, where we
find a great, uninteresting, modern city, hastening
to compete on their own terms with capitals that
have grown slowly, and losing, certainly, all that
gives its character to Moscow.   More significant,
though not meaning precisely what it is generally
taken to mean, is that other saying: "Scratch the
Russian, and you find the Tatar."   It is in no
savage or violent sense that the Russian is still a
civilised barbarian, but in a sense certainly more
profound.

Walking in the streets of Moscow, your first
impression is of something extraordinarily primitive.
The carts which pass you are like the earliest carts
of which you have seen pictures ; by the side of
quite modern trams run little omnibuses, shaped
like the coaches in the museum at St Petersburg ;
the yokes of the horses are made of an immense
hoop of painted wood, unvarying in shape, varying
only in colour.   A man passes silently with a wire-
covered basket on his head, in which he offers
live fowls for sale ; a workman passes, carrying a
wooden spade, and you will notice that his legs
are swathed in rags, his feet covered with sandals
of osier.   Look through the window of a shop,
a bank, and you will see that the reckoning is being
done with Chinese counters.   The very animals,
the dogs and cats, are different from ours.   The
dogs, certainly, are nearer to their wild cousin the

wolf, and gambol with a sort of fierce awkwardness;
while the vast cats walk and lie like tigers. And
the peasants or labourers whom you see in the
streets, in their red and purple and mauve shirts,
with their shaggy beards and tawny hair, cut
neither short nor long, in a straight line all round,
parted in the middle, and standing out wildly on
either side; these large-limbed people, with their
boyish, frank, good-humoured, but untamed faces,
have the faces of beings for whom civilisation does
not exist. The Russian peasant is still the Scythian,
his ancestor. In the Kertch room of the Hermitage
at St Petersburg, in that admirable collection of
Greek remains dating from the fourth and fifth
centuries before Christ, there is a beautiful silver
vase, with griffins, geese, reeds, and conventional
arabesque on its sides; near it are gold ornaments,
thin plaques of gold, worn on dresses, and a smaller
gilt vase. On these you see the Scythians, riding
on horseback, sword in hand; standing back to
back with drawn bow, embracing over a drinking-
horn, pulling out a tooth and bandaging the foot
of a companion; with, on the Nicopolis vase, a
whole series of the episodes of horse-taming.
These Scythian faces are precisely the faces that
you will see in the Russian peasant of to-day, grave,
serious, kindly, with a sort of homely dignity; and,
precisely as in the Russian peasant of to-day, you
will see, in these lively representations of his
ancestor, two thousand years ago, the long shirt,

girt at the waist, and falling half-way to the knees, loose trousers, often tucked into a kind of top-boots; the thick beard, the long hair combed over the forehead.

To see the Muscovite, that is to say the typical Russian, as he really is, observe him on Sunday, and observe him from morning to evening. Sunday in Moscow is a sort of village feast. The shops are shut, but the street markets (beside which the Good Friday fair at the Rialto would seem but pale) are ablaze with buyers and sellers, all in their best clothes; the women looking like big babies in their high-waisted dresses, bright in colour, shapeless in form. All the morning the bells sound overhead, in their loud, muffled buzz, as of a cloud of bronze insects hovering over the city; and the churches are full of devout worshippers, who kiss the sacred ikons, cross themselves in the elaborate manner of the Russian ritual, kneel, and bow till their foreheads touch the ground. As the day goes on an irresponsible animation seems to be in the air; the traktirs are full of tea-drinkers, and by evening vodka has taken the place of tea. The great mechanical organs in the traktirs roll out their set of tunes, voices are heard, joining in the music; and outside the streets are full of gay noise, a song, a quarrel, the slipping of heavy boots over the uncertain pavement; a sort of drunkenness without brutality, a drunkenness which is in the natural course of things, at the natural end of the feast.

The Russian has two devotions: his religion, which is at once an abasement before God and the Tsar, those two omnipotences being more or less identical to him; and his eating and drinking, to which the actual rigours of his climate lend so much importance, and about which he has elaborated a sort of ritual. Between these two devotions very much of his time is taken up. He cannot walk for five minutes along any frequented street without coming upon a church, an ikon, some holy image, a street chapel, an archway under which a sacred lamp burns; and before each of these he must take off his hat, pause, cross himself three times, and make at least two genuflections. His eating and drinking make scarcely less demands upon him. Meals have no definitely fixed hours; tea (the too seductive *tchaï s limon*, tea with lemon) is always waiting. And it is with the solemnity of an act of religion that he is served by the sacristan-like doorkeeper in black and the hieratic waiters in white; silent, attentive ministrants, who incline before him as they hand him his soup or his wine, or collect the coppers which he has left for them on the plate.

Religion, in the unspoilt Russian, the Russian of Moscow or the villages, is not merely an attendance upon strict forms, but a profound sentiment, which in him is the sentiment of duty. It is the simplicity, the completeness, with which he obeys the idea of duty, that has caused officialism and Nihilism, with all the cruelties and disasters and ignorant heroisms

M

which are properly the disease of his over-scrupulous
conscience. You see it in his grave, patient, sensitive
face, in which the soul seems always to look out on
some pathetic inquiry. In the faces of railway
porters and of barefooted peasants who have thronged
the railway stations in remote quarters of Russia, I
have seen the making of martyrs and fanatics. And
they have the gentleness of those who suffer, whom
nature has made for suffering, with a strength which
for the most part is without brutality.

And I think I never saw people so friendly with
one another, except perhaps in Spain; it has become
more than mere friendliness, an earnest helpfulness,
which has stamped itself upon the very faces of the
people. And, after all one has heard of Russian
brutality, it is interesting to note for oneself the
signs of gentleness which are to be found not only
in these grave, bearded, patient faces, but in many
little, unexpected ways. One hardly thinks of Russia
without thinking of the knout. Well, the Russian
cabmen drive without whips, using only the end of
their reins, and the reins finish in a mere bunch of
ribbons.

When the Russian is cruel, he is cruel just as the
barbarian always is, because he is indifferent to pain,
his own or another's. He does not spare, because he
would not complain. And he has the Mohammedan's
readiness to sacrifice everything for a cause; for
him that spiritual and temporal power which is
his religion, and which has taken far deeper root in

him than any mere sentiment, essentially a modern one, of tolerance or of sympathy with suffering. In the Roumiantsof Museum at Moscow there is the cage in which Emilian Pougatchef was imprisoned; it is a cage only very slightly higher and wider than the height and size of an average man; it has chains for fastening hand and foot together, so that the man can only stand upright, without even moving, inside the iron bars of his portable prison. But Pougatchef was a religious revolter, and to spare one who had taken up arms against religion would have been to spare a dangerous enemy of God.

The word which I should use to represent the main impression made on me by the average Russian, the soldier, the railway-porter, the labourer, is uprightness; and it seems to me to contrast very favourably with a quality perhaps equally strong which is to be seen in the face and the bearing of the average German. To the German, discipline and obedience are painful duties; he appreciates them and he acquires them, but he becomes something of an automaton in the process. To the Russian they are the duty which is its own reward, a sort of religion, which it is a delight to fulfil.

The Russian has a genius for self-sacrifice; self-sacrifice has made him a martyr and a conspirator; it has given him strength and weakness. He can resign himself to anything, and resignation can just as easily be heroism or mere apathy. The heroic side of it we all know; the other, at times comic, side, may be

seen any day in the streets of Moscow by watching
a cabman who has been paid too small a fare. He
does not explode into anger, like a cabman in any
other part of the world; he does not contest the
matter, he does not even remonstrate: he looks at
the money in his open hand with a woebegone expression, closes his hand upon it in a gesture of weak
despair, and seems to say, "Well, it has happened
to me again!" Endurance and indifference, apathy
and resignation, are perhaps the natural qualities
called out in the Russian by his struggle with the
elements; heat is his enemy in summer, cold his
enemy in winter. Stirred up by outside influences,
he sometimes fancies that his rulers are also his
enemies; and then he can but devote himself blindly
to the species of new religion which has possessed
itself of his capacity for worship.

But if we would see what is really at the root of
the national character, the actual nature of the
peasant, it is not even in Moscow that it must be
sought, but in such a place as Sergievo, and on such
an occasion as the annual pilgrimage to the Troitsa
Monastery, on the day of the Assumption. The
monastery, bulbous and angular, with its red walls
and gold and green domes and spires, is set on the
triangular point of a small hill; all about it are
bright-coloured sheds and shops and booths, and
little village houses of painted wood; a village fair
was going on, in honour of the pilgrimage, and a
stream of men and women in bright clothes wandered

up and down all the roads incessantly, and gathered
in groups about the tea-shops and the booths of the
fair. Inside the monastery walls, in the churches
and along all the paths, this immense, quiet, ugly
crowd wandered on, or waited patiently at gateways.
It was made up for the most part of women, and
these women were all old, or looked old, and they
were all ugly, and all shapeless, dressed in a patch-
work of bright colours, their skirts looped up about
their red and wrinkled legs, bare to the knee, or
above their osier shoes bound about with cords.
They were shapeless and uncouth, with bodies that
seemed as if they had never known even the animal
joys of life; but there was none of the dirt, disease,
and violence of a French or Italian pilgrimage, of
Lourdes or Casalbordino. They were clean and
sturdy, and they passed slowly, leaning on their
staves, or waiting two and two in long lines, to
enter the church and kiss the relics, with a dogged
patience, without noise, or talking, or laughter;
with a fixed sense of the duty to be done, then of
the need of rest, and then of the long journey home.
They went in order into the large room by the
refectory, took their bread and salt, which they ate
in the refectory, and then sat down, like great grown-
up school children, at long wooden tables, in the
open air, where the monks served them with bread
and soup. Then they flung themselves down on the
ground wherever they happened to find a little free
space, and slept heavily. They lay there with their

heads on their bundles, themselves like big bundles of
rags; some of them lay in the graveyard, upon the
graves and the turf, like a dead army, waiting to be
buried.   And in all this there was no fervour, no
excitement, a perfectly contained emotion, a dogged
doing of something which they had set out to do.
They had come from all parts of Russia, walking all
the way, and they had come simply to kiss the
relics, and then to go home again, because it was
their duty.   They were all good-humoured, cheerful, contented; they accepted discomfort as they
accepted poverty, labour, their bodies which had
never known happiness or beauty.   Contentment
in them was strength, but it had in it also something lamentable.   Here, in this placid and vigorous
herd of animals, were women who had never discovered that women could be beautiful, human
beings who had never discovered that life could be
a desirable thing in itself.

VI

The summer of 1897, they told me in Moscow,
was the hottest summer known there for thirty-
seven years.   I have never suffered so much from heat
in any country of Europe; and Russia, certainly, in
spite of the tempestuous skies, rain, and icy winds
of St Petersburg, will remain in my mind as a
synonym for much that I have imagined of the

tropics. And Moscow is almost without shadow, open to all the oppressions of the sky. Its parks, the Sokolniky, for instance, miles on miles of woods, through which long, dusty roads pierce like high-roads, are without restful corners, are themselves an oppression; you do not see people enjoying the mere fact of being there, as people in Warsaw are seen visibly enjoying the grace and repose of their Watteau-like Saxe Garden; Polish women, with their pale faces and soft hair, their languid activity, coming and going with so constant an appeal to one's sense of delightful things. Here and there, indeed, one finds a corner of the city in which, for a moment, things fall into the attitudes of a picture; and one such space of subdued colour I remember in the Krasny Proud, a great pool near the Iaroslav Station. It was dim grey when I saw it, under morning sun-light, and at the farther edge it was bordered with curdling green, which showed at that distance as a line of delicate, clear green; and the people passing on the bank, their red shirts, the tints of bright waggons, of wooden houses, were reflected in the water. In this harmony, which composed itself naturally, the carts and timber and houses and people all seeming to exist only to be an effect in pale watery colours, I found almost every element of the typical Russian landscape, as I had seen it on my way to Moscow.

But Moscow's most elaborate escape from itself is, to me at least, in the fortified convents, surrounded

with high walls, with embrasures and loop-holes for
cannon, warlike towers at every corner, in which
the monks and nuns used to hold their own against
robbers and Tatars: you still see the cannon, lying
rusty under the porches. The oldest of these
convents is the Novospasky, far off in the east end
of Moscow, near the river and the timber yards. It
was built in the fifteenth century, it holds a bell-
tower and five churches within its walls, among the
trees and garden paths, and some of its mural
paintings are the most tolerable I have seen in
Moscow. But it was the smaller, more central
Strastnoi Convent which gave me the most delightful
sensation, as I found my way into it by chance, one
burning afternoon, as the bell was calling from the
pink church in the midst of the garden, inside the
high pink walls which enclose that little world.
The garden, full of trees and paths, was bordered
by white, one-storeyed houses, out of which nuns and
novices came stealing, in their black habits with
hanging sleeves, the veil tightened around the chin,
under the tall, black, almost Saracen headdress.
Lay sisters were working in the garden-beds, carts
passed slowly along the narrow paths between the
trees, birds sang, grey cats moved quietly about, and
as I sat there, among these placid people, leaning
back against a tree, with a shadow of sunny leaves
above my head, Moscow, its noise and heat, seemed
shut off as by a veil of quiet, the deep buzz of the
bell overhead being but like the sound which is

nearest to silence in a summer forest; and the
world seemed once more a place of possible rest, in
which it was not needful to hurry through the
sunshine.

Summer, 1897.

BUDAPEST, BELGRADE, AND
SOFIA

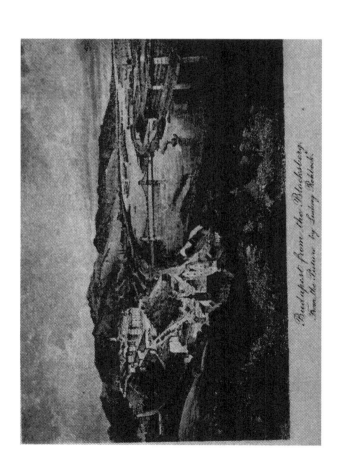

Budapest from the Blocksberg.
From the Picture by Ludwig Rohbock.

BUDAPEST, BELGRADE, AND SOFIA

I

BUDAPEST

In Budapest there is nothing but what the people and a natural brightness in the air make of it. Here things are what they seem; atmosphere is everything, and the atmosphere is almost one of illusion. Budapest lives, with a speed that thrusts itself, not unattractively, upon one at every moment. Think of your first impressions of the place and they will be all of one kind: the porter who snatches your luggage from you, runs at full speed, and dives under the horses' heads; the electric trams that dash through the streets, the swift two-horse cabs; the bite of paprika in the food; the unusual glitter and pungency of the brass bands, and the gipsy fiddlers with their fiddles and bodies alive all over. The people with their sombre, fiery, and regular faces have the look of sleepy animals about to spring. Go into a café and, as you sit at your table, you will see every eye turned quietly, fixedly, upon you, with an insistence in which there is no insolence. Coming from Austria, you seem, since you have left Vienna, to have crossed more than a frontier. You are in another world, in which people live with a more vivid and a quite incalculable life : the East has begun.

The main streets of Budapest are broad Austrian streets, tall and showy ; but they open at every moment into long, winding, narrow streets, which again open through side passages into squares, surrounded by galleries ; shops and inns are hidden away there, waggons and bales of goods stand in the midst ; and the inner life of the city seems to withdraw itself into these obscure corners. To the stranger, Budapest hardly exists beyond the Ferencz-Josef Rampart along the river, which has at all hours an operatic air, as of something hastily got up for your pleasure, and with immense success. Well-dressed people walk to and fro upon this cheerful boulevard, with its trees, cafés, and flags ; little trams run smoothly along it between you and the water, with a continual, not unpleasant, agitation ; steamers pass on the river. At sunset every point of the abrupt hill opposite is detailed in sharp silhouette against a glowing sky, out of which the colour is about to fade ; the whole uninteresting outline of the palace, seen under this illumination, becomes beautiful. Lights begin to star the two hills, the hill of the citadel and the hill of the palace, sparkling out of the darkness like glow-worms ; lights come out along the bridge and strike the water like gold swords. Some charm is in the air, and a scarcely definable sense of pleasure, which makes one glad to be there. One has been suddenly released from the broad spaces, empty heights, and tiring movement of Vienna, in which, to the stranger, there is only the mechanical part of gaiety and only the pretentious part of seriousness. Here, in Budapest, it is delightful to be a stranger; it is as if a door had been thrown open, and one found oneself at home with bright strangenesses. Idleness becomes active; there is no need for thought, and no inclination to think beyond the passing moment.

Only a few steps away from this very self-conscious, very civilised, though singularly foreign life and movement, you will find another, stranger, more primitive centre of life. The fruit market along the quay, at the end of the town, gave me the first sensation of an opulent natural force of the earth, which one looks for under these less temperate skies. Heaped all over the ground, in piles and pyramids, overflowing from vast baskets, brimming over the sides of carts, multitudes of plums, grapes, peaches, apples, pears, melons, with some fiery-coloured vegetables, glowed in the sunlight. They were all monstrous in size, and they seemed to be squandered idly by some spendthrift prodigality of nature. Among these abnormal fruits, peasants, dressed in many different costumes, cried and shouted in a tangle of dialects. There were women with hooped petticoats swaying about their prodigious legs, and above their small feet with no ankles;

there were men in sheepskin coats, and baggy trousers, and Astrakhan caps; and the air jangled with harsh sounds, and quivered with crude colours, as they moved to and fro, unlading their carts and carrying their heavy baskets and chaffering in unintelligible tongues.

People go to Budapest, and rightly, to hear the gipsy music, as it can be heard only in Hungary; but I was curious to hear the music which was to be heard in the theatres, and to see a little acting and dancing. "A Kereszt jelében," or " The Sign of the Cross," was being given at one of the theatres, but I preferred the programme at the Opera: " Bajazzók," or "I Pagliacci," and a ballet called " Szerelmi Kaland," or " Histoire d'Amour." The orchestra at the opera was not good, and the Hungarian language does not seem to set itself easily to music. Some of the singers were content with shouting hoarsely, as they acted with a kind of stilted savagery. And the acting was something like Spanish acting, all jerks and snaps; with, at times, a quaint suggestion of the Japanese, but without their genius for being animals. The ballet was much better done; it was done lightly, with pleasant humour, with a delicious sense of gaiety. The *corps de ballet* was younger and prettier than it usually is on the continent, and the girls danced as if it were natural to them to dance, with their hands and arms as well as with their feet. It was a *ballet-fantaisie*, and the style seemed to suit the place and

the people. I have not often seen a chahut done
with such spirit, or with so natural an extravagance.

I remember, when I was in Budapest before, seeing a ballet in which there was a certain amount of
local colour; it was, I think, the ballet called
"Csárdás." The true local colour in music, however, has to be sought in the cafés, or wherever
gipsies play Hungarian music. The Hungarian
gipsies are the most naturally musical people in the
world. Music is their instinctive means of expression; they do not learn it, it comes to them of itself.
Go into a roadside tent in Hungary, and you will see
a little boy of four stretched naked upon the ground,
holding a violin in his arms and drawing his bow
across it, trying to make it speak. The leader of a
band is usually able to read from note; the others
follow his lead, picking up a whole composition with
astonishing rapidity. It is true that they play like
men who have never been trained, gaining something
in naïveté and abandon for what they lose in
mechanical precision. The gipsies hold their violin
in almost every position but the normal one : against
the middle of the chest, on the shoulder near the
ear, on the knee. Their fingering is elementary ;
they use the bow sometimes as a hammer, sometimes
as a whip; they pluck at the strings with all their
fingers at once, as if they would tear the heart out
of the tormented fiddle. And, indeed, it is the heart
that cries and sobs, and is happy and exults, in the
joyful agonies of the csárdás. The time varies, the

rhythm fantastically disguised by a prolonged vibra-
tion, as it were, of notes humming round a central
tone. In its keen intensity and profuse ornamentation, an arabesque of living flame, it is like nothing
else in music. And in this unique effect the national
instrument, the czimbalom, counts for much. The
czimbalom consists of a framework of wires fixed on
a sort of table. The wires are struck by flexible
quills, padded at the end, which are held one in each
hand. The little soft hammers rise and fall, and flit
to and fro with incredible swiftness, in a sort of
effervescence of sound.

In Budapest there is a gipsy band in every café,
and as you walk along the streets at night you will
hear at every moment the scrape of fiddles from behind curtained and lighted windows. Gipsy bands
play in the hotels every evening, till after midnight;
sometimes under the leadership of a cultivated artist,
like Berkes Béla, who has money of his own, and
is supposed to play for pleasure on his admirable
Stradivarius. The leader, standing with his back to his
men, and turning half round to them as he indicates
a sudden change of time, plays away with his whole
body; he rises to the tips of his toes, bends, crouches
as if about to spring, sways as if in a great wind.
This music, I think, is after all scarcely music; but
rather nerves, a suspense, a wheeling of wings around
a fixed point. In this mournfulness, this recoil and
return, there is a kind of spring and clutch; a native
wildness speaks in it, as it speaks in the eyes of these

dark animals, with their look of wild beasts eying
their keepers. It is a crushed revolt, and it cries out
of a storm, and it abandons itself after the lament to
an orgy of dancing. It is tigerish, at once wild and
stealthy. And it draws everything into its own net.
Listen to the Hungarian as he translates the music
of other countries into his own half-oriental language.
The slangy American tunes assume a new character,
a certain lively brilliance, no longer vulgar. Even
English tunes forget to be common in their sentimentality, and become full of languorous tenderness,
into which a drop of fire has dripped. Hungarian
gipsy music is a music full of surprises, always turning along unexpected ways; the music of a race
whose roots are outside Europe. And in the playing of the Hungarian gipsies there is the same finish,
the same finesse, as in their faces, so regular, and so
full of fire under a semblance of immobility.

II

BELGRADE

The sunset sky, against which I first saw Belgrade,
was like a crimson and orange and purple moth, barred
with colours as hard and clear as enamel. Belgrade
stood heaped white on its hill, all its windows on fire
with light; a long white mound, set there in a semi-
circle above water and a great plain, with a point of

land running down into the water. Beyond the city,
as you enter Servia, there are valleys in which the
trees grow as thick as grass, bulrushes tufted with
white wool along the river-courses, great fields of
melons, with their dry stalks, and often a kind of
English scenery, a monotony of tilled plenty. You
come upon cottages, surrounded by a hedge of plaited
wood ; villages, with square, brown-roofed huts, the
roofs edged with white, set in the midst of trees ; a
little town, into which several villages seem to have
joined themselves, with its white square church with
a red dome. The soil is rich and varied, seeming to
yield itself willingly to cultivation. Delicate trees,
which I saw when they were yellow and fired with
autumn, grow everywhere in irregular clusters. The
green and brown plain spreads outwards, full of trees
and meadows, long lines and thick squares of trees
with meadows between, and a barrier of low hills all
round. Servia is a land of contrasts, and beyond
Stalatz, where the two Moravas meet, wooded gorges
begin, gradually turning to barer and barer rock.
The train cuts through the mountains and skirts the
bottom of ravines, tracing its line parallel with the
streams. Walls of grey granite go straight up into
the hard, blue sky, which you can just see above
their summits. Even here there is not the savagery
of Bulgaria, which the land resembles a little. The
great gorge between Nisch and Zaribrod, which may
be compared with the Dragoman Pass between Zaribrod and Sofia, is far finer ; it is at once bolder and

more shapely, cut more finely by nature, and coloured more sensitively.

Belgrade reminded me at one time of Moscow, at another of some white Spanish city. The whole place is made by the crossing of straight lines: I never saw a curve. Few of the houses have more than two storeys; the streets are broad, mountainously paved; and when I came into it at night there was a white nocturnal silence over everything. There were few lights, few people passing; but by the roadside I saw two gipsies crouching, their faces almost black, the woman's splendid in profile. There are trees in almost all the streets, avenues leading into the open country all round; and, at evening, just as the lights were lit, queer chattering birds like crows began bustling and talking overhead in a language that I have never heard before among birds. Oxen, with huge branching horns, move slowly through the streets, drawing long, narrow wooden carts; or lie down to rest, as the men do at midday, with their heads on the stones with which they are paving the streets. The town is like a great village, ready made; and one can imagine it being harnessed to those oxen, and carted bodily away, and the flat, dreary country which lies all round relapsing into its original dry barrenness.

Yet the place is thriving, and has been so for some twenty years. It is full of merchants, who come to buy plums and eggs and coal; they rush into the restaurant of the Grand Hotel for lunch,

eat hastily, and rush out again, much as men do
in the city. There are new streets, uninterestingly
new, among the older streets, not old enough to be
interesting. In the older streets you see the admirable peasant things, sheepskins, furs, white serge
coats and trousers, hanging at the windows and doorways of the shops in which they are made; in the
newer streets the shops are filled with hideous,
cheap, modern finery. There is one excellent
bookshop, in which I saw French and English
books: Verlaine's " Choix de Poésies," Mallarmé's
" Poésies," the French version of Nietzsche's " Also
sprach Zarathustra," Mrs Meynell's "Ruskin." There
is a new theatre, which, when I was there, was lit up
for " Magda." Close by is a dingy and half-empty
café, in which a few women in music-hall dresses
sing music-hall songs ; and farther on a sad-faced
Damen-Capelle, playing stringed instruments. Few
people are in the streets after dark; only, at intervals,
one hears the slow creaking of the bullock-carts and
the clatter of wheels over the stony roads ; and,
overhead, the high-slung gas globes, at long dis-
tances from one another, start, splutter, go out, and
come to life again.

On the edge of the hill, looking over the plain,
the river, and Zimony is a dreary little park, the
Kalemegdan, which comes out on a broad terrace
planted with thin and sickly trees, each with its
little circle of parched flowers around the root.
Late at night the park becomes mysterious, with

its few gas lamps, the thick darkness under the trees, which creak slowly, the little turning fountain glittering in a thin pattern in the air, the glimpse down dim alleys, out of which I once saw two peasants, dressed in red and brown and white clothes, like two Giorgione figures, stroll slowly from the darkness and back into the darkness. People walk on the terrace just before sunset, as the sun goes down across a wide, flat, dreary plain, with many waters winding through it, cutting sharp patterns in the soil, and broadening out almost to the aspect of a lake. Below, to the left, are factories, roofs, and chimneys rising out of the hill, and below that the wharf and the small steamers. After the sun has set the river grows colder and paler, and the short grass of the plain turns to exactly the colour and texture of the Infanta's green velvet dress in Velasquez's picture at Vienna. On the right the river sweeps broadly towards Zimony; you see its spires against a sky which reddens through trailing smoke; and, in those moments' effect, in that severe harmony of light and smoke and water, a curious and doubtful charm grows up out of the literal dreariness of things.

If it were not for the peasants and the gipsies Belgrade would be a provincial capital and no more; but the Servian gipsies are remarkable even among gipsies, and the Servian peasants are sometimes like savage chiefs, sometimes like ancient Greeks, with their fine, dark, regular faces, black eyes and hair, straight slim figures, and wonderful clothes. Their clothes are for the most part white; long white sack-like coats, and white short sheepskin coats, with the soft fleece inside, the untanned hide embroidered in cunning lines and circles of black and red; large, loose, baggy, white trousers pulled in at the ankle, heavily embroidered stockings and belts, waistcoats of embroidered leather, Astrakhan caps formed into conical points, and shoes of white leather, made like sandals. The women are not often so handsome; the peasants wear embroidered leather coats like the men, and embroidered heavy skirts and stockings; but the townswomen wear short coats of black velvet and black satin, with hanging sleeves and gold edges; their hair is plaited round a tight red skull cap, which shows through the hair, and, below, ribbons are drawn across like fillets, and these are hung with trinkets and fastened with great gold pins. The "better classes" dress hideously, as near the Paris fashions as they can, and may be seen walking in the streets, accompanied by their maids in the admirable native costume. The peasant women carry long staves with several notches, which they put over their shoulders, and on which they sling cans and baskets. You will see three young girls, thus loaded, each with a different coloured handkerchief over her head, each with her red embroidered skirt looped gracefully on either side, showing a white embroidered petticoat, embroidered stockings,

and soft padded shoes. As I look out of the window
of the hotel I see four old women with yellow handkerchiefs and red skirts, one with a brilliant apron of
red and yellow, who have laid down their burdens
and are sitting on the ground at the corner of the
little square.   Men are repaving the square in a
slow, primitive fashion ; the bullock-carts come and
go with loads of stones, and stand outside the front
door of the hotel as if they were in their own village.

But it is in the market that one is best able to
study the peasants and the gipsies.   The market is
held on some open ground under the trees, not far
from the theatre ; and the whole ground is piled up
with fruits and vegetables of all colours, of vast
sizes, and in profuse abundance.   Women and girls
stand gravely beside their coloured heaps, not seeming
to care if they are bought or not, but chaffering
eagerly over every sale.   They stand there, in twos
and threes, bundled up in their multitudes of skirts
and vests, with their hands folded over their
stomachs; young and old hardly at first sight dis-
tinguishable; all with their great gilt buckles at the
waist, their necklaces of glass beads, their many
rings, their kerchiefed heads, often hung with coins
and flowers and green leaves.   Fine savage old men
in tatters wander about the outskirts of the market,
all brown wrinkles; I saw one who seemed as if
dressed in armour; for his leather jerkin had gone
hard and black with age, and clasped him like a
gorget.   Some of the women have lovely and quite

regular faces, and delicately cut mouths and noses,
level black eyelids and sullen eyes high up under
them. But the gipsies! I had seen one old
woman, an animal worn to subtlety, with the cunning
of her race in all her wrinkles, trudging through the
streets with a kind of hostile gravity. But here it
was the children who fascinated me. There were
three little girls, with exactly the skin of Hindus,
and exactly the same delicately shaped face, and
lustrous eyes, and long dark eyelashes; and they
followed me through the market, begging in strange
tongues, little cat-like creatures full of humour,
vivacity, and bright instinctive intelligence. As we
came to one end of the market, they ran up to a
young girl of about fifteen, who stood leaning against
a pump. She was slender, with a thin, perfectly
shaped face, the nose rather arched, the eyes large,
black, lustrous, under her black eyelids ; thick masses
of black hair ran across her forehead, under the
scarlet kerchief. She leaned there, haughty, magnetic,
indifferent ; a swift animal, like a strung bow, bringing all the East with her, and a shy wildness which
is the gipsy's only.

III

SOFIA

The soil of Bulgaria is a dry and barren soil,
coloured for the most part a sickly pink, and mixed

with rocks, rising into irregular hills, on which there
is sometimes a scanty growth of small trees. Sometimes the colour of the soil turns to faded lavender;
lavender rocks lie about in great splinters. It is a
harsh unnatural land, cursed with barrenness. Dry
water-courses have moulded their beds at the
bottom of scooped-out gorges; there are long flat
spaces of dreary sand and stone; everywhere un-
lovely outlines, sombre colours, a desperate and
lonely wildness. In one of the gorges, through
which runs a tiny trickle of water, you will see
sheep, black and white, by hundreds, which have
come down from the uplands to drink, or some
buffaloes coming rapidly down a steep path, or a
company of gipsies who have made their camp there,
and are lighting a fire in a hollow of the rocks.
Beyond Sofia the land changes; there is a continual
interchange of luxuriance and savagery, in the
sharpest contrasts I have ever seen. The hills are
cut abruptly into rough shapes blotting out the
sky; here and there you see a few buffaloes, a flock
of sheep with their shepherd, inside a circle of
thorns; or a man casting seed out of a bag into
brown furrows, or a man in a sheepskin coat riding
down a steep road. There are hills covered deep
with trees, then bare hills again, the vast rocks, dry
earth, and cavernous ravines of the Dragoman Pass.

Sofia is like a town set down in the midst of a
great desert. Wandering out on every side, one
comes first to a kind of village, and then to a desert,

dusty endings not without a desolate charm. Hills rim the plain in which the town with its trees lies like a somewhat dreary oasis. The plain is wide and barren, with a few trees and a few red-roofed cottages; beyond, the great hills, cut into soft, dark, rugged cliffs and curves, spreading up nakedly out of the plain into the sky. From the higher ground you see the whole plain with the town in its midst. Low, flat houses, with only here and there a dome or turret, but intersected by many tall and straight trees, lie tightly pressed together; the walls are painted red, green, and white, and a wooden paling seems to run round the whole long and narrow mass. As one takes the first step outside this paling, it is as if a gate had shut suddenly behind one, shutting in the town. Telegraph wires stretch across the plain, but the buffalo carts come down from the hills, and the pack horses trudge up towards them, and the peasants sit on the ground, resting by the way, and the black and white geese cackle among the sedge, and there is always dust blowing and a rustling of wind among the weedy grasses.

There is something dry, hot, and fierce in this place, which is at once ordinary, sordid, and almost startling. It is a place at once violent and sullen, in which everything is dusty and dingy and half-used or half-finished. Stones and building materials lie strewn in the streets, houses are being made and houses are falling into ruins; everything is crude, sordid, with a crudity and sordidness which are half-

western and half-eastern, and made out of the worst
elements of both. The houses are for the most part
such houses as one might see in any small town in
any country, but at a corner of the main street there
is a mosque, and around the mosque something like
a village fair. Wooden booths are set up at each
side of the street, wooden palings surround empty
spaces or open upon cafés in which trees grow, or
upon one-storey houses, or upon a little wooden
theatre. Money-changers, with their glass cases of
gold and silver coins, and coin-earrings, and rings,
outside their shop windows, suggest already the
sarafs of Constantinople. At upper windows above
the shops you see men working sewing-machines;
at the edge of the pavement little dark boot-blacks,
Kurds, sit with their wooden blocks before them.
Men pass selling water, grapes, and nuts; a woman
passes, and then another, carrying a huge dark green
melon in her arms, solemnly, like a royal orb. Men
stand about at the street corners in rags of all colours,
sewn together in all fashions; there is something
sordid and savage in these brutal faces, these huddled
figures, this slouching gait, in this boisterous language
with its jerks and splutters, in the barbarous clash of
costumes, in all this idleness, suspicion, this mingling
of elements that do not unite, this hostility of races,
seen in the mere coming and going of the people;
together with an odd sense of provinciality, as you
meet processions with bands, carrying coloured flags,
like friendly societies in England, and walking through

the streets in step, singing solemn tunes like hymn-tunes.

On Sunday, Sofia takes on something preposterously like the aspect of an English Sunday. The shops are shut, the people put on their best clothes, and lounge in the streets, or sit on the rustic wooden benches in the park (the one restful place in Sofia, with its quaint acacias, its tiny fountain, its wholly natural and unspoilt aspect), or walk out to the Boris Gardens, a mile beyond the town. As I fell into the steady and unending procession of people, one Sunday which was also a national fête, it seemed to me that the town had emptied itself, as a Spanish town empties itself on the day of a bullfight. Men and women of all classes walked slowly and steadily along side by side, in a kind of orderly jumble. I watched the peasants, and found them less attractive than the peasants of Servia, both in themselves and in their costume. They are tall and strong, but they have something common, sullen, and slouching, which is not in the Servians, and they do not dress so well, though they dress distinctively and with effect. The costume of the women is crude, with its black and orange, its reds and gold, its narrow black petticoat covered with a bright apron, its sequins about the neck, its red handkerchief wrapped round the head and twisted into the plaits of hair falling down the back. The men wear white serge trousers, not so baggy as in Servia, braided slightly in black, a white shirt embroidered in red or bound with black braid,

a black or brown jacket coming to the waist, with a
sort of flap falling over behind, and a brown or black
round fur cap; a red sash wound about the waist,
and often, outside, one of the sheepskin coats which
I had seen in Servia. Side by side with the peasants there were Turks wearing the fez, indistinguishable people of indistinguishable nationalities, and
very commonplace townsfolk, who presently took
part in the most childish sports I have ever seen, or
stood in excited rings watching them, or danced in
circles, with clasped hands and hopping feet, like
English soldiers in camp.

At night Sofia returns to itself, or to what is more
dubious and unfamiliar in itself. Sounds of music
and voices come from behind doors and curtained
windows; doors swing open upon a glimpse of
strangely dressed musicians on a platform, a woman
standing singing, peasants sitting or moving about
the room. In the main street there is an open-air
café, with little tables under the trees, and lights
swung across from tree to tree. Ten or twelve men
sit on a raised and covered platform in one corner,
dressed in white trousers and dark-blue embroidered
coats and white embroidered shirts; the leader plays
on a flute, and the others on fiddles, a 'cello, a
double-bass, a cornet, a big drum, cymbals, and
some instruments which seem like children's toys.
These, I discovered, were used for producing imita-
tive effects, when the orchestra did its best to
reproduce the sounds of a railway-train or a fire-

engine: the noise and rattle always ended in something very like a hymn. It was the music of people not naturally musical, and without any restraining education in music.

I went away from the café discontentedly, and, turning out of the main street, I heard a lugubrious sound, half cry and half shriek, with a muttering of dull and shrill instruments, coming from behind a wooden paling. I went in and sat down at a table under the trees. Short grimy posts, hardly higher than my head, standing like dirty dwarfs among the acacias, held up big oil lamps made after the pattern of the gas lamps in the streets of London; at the end of the courtyard there was an open window in a trellised wall, through which a serving man handed out beer and coffee to the waiters. Opposite to the entrance there was a covered platform, as in the other café. In front were four girls dressed in gaudy Turkish costume, seated on chairs, with one or two men and women in plain clothes at their side. Behind were the musicians, who plucked at stringed instruments with their fingers or with a kind of brass thimble, beat on a tambourine and a little drum, and blew into a long flute. The aspect of the stage reminded me of Spain, and recalled the "Chinitas" at Malaga; and the music and dancing had a distinct kinship with Spanish music and dancing. What I saw and heard was partly Turkish and partly Hungarian; there was the csárdás, and there was the *danse du ventre*. And there were also those

interminable, piercing, disturbing Eastern songs
which have so much in them of the Malagueña.
The *danse du ventre*, done by a Greek in a kind
of uniform covered with gold lace, and wearing a
long ivory-handled sword, and by an Armenian girl
in a white vest and green trousers, was the most
elaborate pantomime of sex that I have ever seen;
it made a kind of art of obscenity. It is the same
drama as the drama of Spanish dancing, but it is
more explicit, and it is done as if it were something
amusing, a game, and not, as with the Spaniard, a
struggle, an irresistible appeal, an agony. In that
dance I realised the whole difference between the
consciousness of the East and what seems to us
most like the Eastern point of view among Western
nations. A kind of mongrel East was visibly upon
me, and I felt that it would be only one more step
to Constantinople.

And yet that one step, I realised, would mean
everything. What is so disquieting in Sofia is that
it lies between two civilisations, and that it is a kind
of rag-heap for the refuse of both. The main street
of Sofia is the most horrible street in Europe. You
see first of all mere European frippery, tin pots and
pans, scraps of leather, shoes and slippers hanging
from nails in front of shops, gimcracks in china,
knives, "fancy articles," none personal to the place;
rows of second-hand books and pamphlets, mostly in
Russian (I saw "Anna Karénina," Tourguenieff's
"Faust," Gorki's "Tchelkache," a life of Shake-

o

speare and of Benjamin Franklin), and along with them,
strung upon upright boards by strings, cheap photographs of actresses, Cavalieri, or Cléo de Mérode,
and sentimental German photographs; then stalls of
fruit, powdered thick with dust, dust-covered loaves
of bread, which looked like great stones, crescents
of sausages, coloured greenish red, trays and dishes
of hot messes cooked over little ovens in the road;
but above all meat: carcasses stripped of the hide,
with their tails still hanging, the horns and hide
lying outside in the gutter; beasts hacked in two,
from which joints are being cut; everywhere yellow
meat hanging from chains; all smells and all colours,
as of the refuse of a slaughter-house. Men pass you
on the pavement carrying the bodies of dead beasts
upon their shoulders; you see a huddle of blood-
stained hides in a cart standing beside the pavement; ducks and chickens squeak and flutter as
they writhe head downwards under men's arms.
And there is a continual coming and going of
peasants in ragged and coloured clothes, women
and girls with negress-like faces, wearing Turkish
trousers under a sort of apron, half-naked gipsy
children darting hither and thither, merchants,
casual Europeans, in bowlers and overcoats; and,
all the time, the rattle of the electric trams in the
street as they pass to and fro, with their mockery
of progress, through this city of dust and rags.

AUTUMN, 1902.

CONSTANTINOPLE

Constantinople.
From the Picture by W. Millerp

CONSTANTINOPLE

I

WATER, camels, sand, then broader water, boats, a littie station, with a veiled woman standing in a doorway; then more water and sandy grass, a few trees, then waste land, a long line of bullocks ploughing; then, between the railway and the water, a cluster of coloured houses, mostly of wood; then trees, more waste land, a little bay, with hills beyond; then fields, more clusters of mean houses, ploughed land, and water; at last, the wall, with its gaps and towers; a graveyard, gardens; then, between roofs and walls, the long curve of Constantinople. A dense smell, dogs, houses, then an actual seashore, with men wading bare-legged in the water, and boats coming in laden with melons; then streets of houses, with fragments of turreted walls, two birds on every turret; side-streets, cutting deeply between two lines of low red roofs; faces of many colours, strange clothes; then, over the roofs, but close, the water, houses, domes, minarets of the city, in a flash, veiled suddenly by the walls of the station, fastened about one.

II

At the end of my first day in Constantinople I find myself bewildered, as if I have lost my way in my own brain. I seem to have been blown through a whirlwind, out of which I can clutch nothing tangible. I recall the drive from the station, near midday, through dense, moving, red-capped crowds, an angry mob, as it seemed, surging . about one, each going his own way, heedlessly and violently. I tried to catch every detail, as it changed before me; to fix my attention and my memory upon a fluid spectacle. The timbers of the bridge creaked and pitched under me; these unintelligible figures came towards me, passed, went on their way; and beyond them, on both sides of me, lay the water, a knotted forest of masts along the quays, from which caiques glided outwards; in front, tier above tier, Galata, the tower, the new town Pera. Walking back in the afternoon, down unpaved cataracts of streets, across the torrent of the bridge, I found myself again in Stamboul. I remember lifting a chain to pass under one of the gateways into the Bazaar, the negro woman wrapped in a bright green mantle who squatted there, only her black face visible, the droning voice of a beggar reciting the Koran; and then the narrow lanes, hung with frippery, the dirty mountainous paths under painted arches, crossing one another in a jungle of gaudy hedges. Then I can remember only a confused mingling of hamals, bent double under mountainous weights; the tall black hats and black cassocks of Armenian priests, the plaited turbans of Arabs, the thin black crape over the faces of veiled women, hooded in dominoes; and, everywhere, the dogs, lying in the roads and on the pavements, meek, sickly creatures, like poor relations, only asking not to be trodden on.

To walk, in Constantinople, is like a fierce and active struggle. One should look at once before, behind, and underneath one's feet; before, behind, and underneath one's feet some danger or disgust is always threatening. I never walked up the steep road which leads from the bridge to Pera without the feeling that I was fighting my way through a hostile city. A horn blows furiously, and a black man runs up the hill, clearing the way before the dashing and struggling horses of the tram. At the same moment a cab drives at full speed down the hill, and the horses set their feet on the pavement. In front of you a man balances slices of offal on a long pole across his shoulder; they dangle before and behind; he swings cheerfully with his burden through the crowd. A Kurd stooping under a weight higher than himself follows step by step behind you. Your feet slip in slushy mud, and catch on the cobbles or in the gaps of the road. A dog with a red wound behind his ear, and a long strip of mangy skin on his back lies asleep in the middle of the pavement. You step into the road to avoid the dogs and the hamals, and wheels and horses are upon you. You step back into the midst of the dogs and the hamals; as you stand aside for a moment, a beggar with a handless arm rounded into a stump, a woman with her face eaten away in the cavity of the hood which she draws back before you, appears suddenly, filling what had seemed the only alley of escape. The sun soaks down into the narrow street, the smell of the mud rises up into your nostrils, mingled with those unknown smells which, in Constantinople, seem to ooze upwards out of the ground and steam outwards from every door and window, and pour out of every alley, and rise like a cloud out of the breath and sweat and foulness of the people.

Cross either of the bridges, and you must look not less carefully to your feet. The old bridge hangs by a thread; it was broken in two, and has never been mended, only patched; in the middle, where it is some inches narrower, an iron-plated barge supports it. It sways, creaks, catches your feet, seems at every moment about to fall·abroad into the water, which you see through the holes in its planks. The railing is held together by iron wire, the ends of the beams hang out ragged and broken over the water. The Grand Pont is more solidly based, but it is made of rough planks set together in irregular lengths and at uneven levels, nailed roughly, the nails standing up out of the planks. It is always in course of making; planks lie about in the road, waiting for use; men are working above great gaps, through which you see the water. As wheels rattle over it, the planks leap up under your feet; you can scarcely set foot on a plank that is not quivering. On each side is a narrow side-walk, slightly raised, and clamped at the edge with iron. A cross current drives at you as you walk along it; people are crowding up and down from the steamboats of the Bosphorus and the Golden Horn, which have their quays moored to the right and left of the bridge. Wheels are upon you from every side; there is no rule of the road; every one fights his own way through for himself.

The main street of Constantinople is the Grande Rue de Péra. I went into it first at night; there were but few shops open, a few men sitting on the chairs outside the cafés, a few passers. Heaps of refuse lay in the gutters, dogs nosed into the refuse, dogs lay asleep in all the holes and jags of the pavement. As I passed, a strange dog was being led in leash through their midst, and a howling began which was caught up and continued along the street; dog after dog got up slowly, and began to bark; there was a dense, uninterrupted noise, which I soon came to know as the unresting, inarticulate voice of the city.

Earlier in the evening at the six o'clock promenade, the Grande Rue de Péra is filled with people. There are a few Turks sitting at the cafés, tranquilly, with their cigarettes, watching the passers; poor men sit at the street corners, sweating and idle; hamals pass, staggering under burdens, grape-sellers weighed down with deep hampers of grapes; tawdry shops are open, with dark young men lounging in the doorways; the red fez passes, with the distrustful, disdainful, anxious eyes under it; but for the most part, in this crush and tangle of races, each elbowing the other in the slime of the street, and against the shoulder of the trotting tram-horse, it is the European that one sees, the Levantine, the Greek, the Armenian, women and young girls, dark, with profound eyes and empty faces, tightened into their smart dresses, walking slowly, cynically, with their free, hard, roving eyes; young girls with superb hair and finely cut mouths and neat, small, firm figures; men with handsome, deceitful faces, odiously regular and lustrous; a slow, steady passing, uncomfortable and continuous.

III

Stamboul, seen from the old bridge at evening, goes up like a mountain to the domes and lances of the Suleimanié. It lies with its feet in the water, like Venice; out of the water rise brown masts and spars, with furled sails, the lines fitting together into exquisite patterns; and this great, dim, coloured mass, in which certain dull reds, greys, and faint blues catch the eye, harmonises into a kind of various brown, like some rich, veined wood. It is set, like Rome, on seven hills, each with its mosque, tower, or monumental ruin; at Seraglio Point it steps into the Sea of Marmora, at the mouth of the Bosphorus, looking across at Asia; it stands between water and water, with the Sea of Marmora at its back, and the Golden Horn at its feet. Every conquest which has swept over it has left a ruin or a monument on its heights. Santa Sophia and the Mosque of Ahmed stand where the Hippodrome once stood; the Burnt Column, its porphyry cracked and hooped and darkened, stands, still upright, where Constantine set it; the broken aqueduct of Valens still stretches across the city to Eyoub; the Mosque of Suleiman and the Mosque of Mahomet V. crown the two hills where the two conquerors built them; and you can follow the walls on the same track which Constantine followed, when he planned the city which was to rule the East.

The streets of Stamboul climb and zigzag; to walk in them is to crawl like a maggot in rotting cheese. A tram runs along one winding road, distracting it with a little civilisation. Away from the tram-line, and even along part of it, Stamboul is Eastern; the Thousand and One Nights are not yet over. The Bazaar lies in its midst, a centre of

leisurely and vehement life; around the Bazaar
there are streets of shops, in which men live and
work according to their trades: I remember best
the street of the shoemakers and the street of the
workers in iron. Markets spread outwards and
downwards, and, level with the quays, there are
more populous streets of shops, in which men
make wooden and iron things for the ships, and
clothes for those who come and go in the ships;
and there is always a quayside bustle, smell, and
filth; fierce men shouldering along, and sore dogs,
and men with red scarves round their heads, sitting
on stools smoking cigarettes and drinking coffee out
of tiny cups. Through openings between the sheds
and houses you can see ships being loaded, mended,
and painted; caiques wait to take passengers across,
and the passengers sit in the caiques with umbrellas
over their heads.

As you climb from either bridge, and turn this
way and that among side streets, you pass into
silence, and a disturbing emptiness of life. The
houses are all blind, the doors fast, the windows
grated over with wooden gratings, which reach two-
thirds up the window, above which an unwashed
blind hangs awry. The houses are made of unpainted wood; they are flat, or the second storey is
set cornerwise on the first; and they are put
together like cupboards, often very neatly, sometimes with a little carving around the panels of the
door. They are all made on much the same pattern,

the door usually in the left-hand corner, the windows
set with studied irregularity, each square or oblong;
they have the air of dolls' houses. No one seems
to go in or out, not a blind quivers, not a glimmer is
seen through the wooden grating; rarely a sound
comes through. Life is hidden away there secretly;
at watch, perhaps, behind the grating; barred in, as
if into a convent or a prison. Close to them, around
a corner, or at their feet, life boils and bubbles;
there is fierce colour, gesture, though little noise,
among people who walk and move gravely. As a
stranger passes, all eyes turn on him, with that
doubtful, not hostile, but ready to be hostile look
which I have come to know so well.

With sunset all the life of Stamboul dies out
suddenly, like the light in the sky. I had been
standing in the great square of the Seraskierat,
watching the orange fire fade slowly at the end of a
narrow street, where it filled the little space of sky.
The light dwindled off the high Oriental gateway,
and the walls and domes and minarets of the
Bajazidié, the mosque of pigeons, darkened by its
cypresses. It was through a changed aspect of
things that I walked back, following the tram-line
which winds about, past the Burnt Column, and
the At-Meidan Square, and Santa Sophia, and
the Sublime Porte, and the outer walls of the
Old Serai, down to the tumultuous square by the
bridge. Dark came on rapidly, but I still saw the
glitter of the Sea of Marmora, down one or two

side streets, as if at the end of the street. Faint gas lamps began to flicker feebly, showing one here and there a gap in the road, a heap of refuse, a dog with all its sores laid out across one's path. Carriages passed at intervals, dashing from side to side of the road with a clatter of hoofs and a rattling of wheels. Many of the dogs rose slowly from the gutter and began a fierce barking; the uneasiness of the night had come upon them. Light shone out of open windows and from behind closed blinds; fierce, half-seen figures passed rapidly; a few men still sat on the little chairs in the road, where they had been drinking coffee, and still sucked, like babies with bottles, at the long tubes of their narghilehs. Some of them were those patriarchal Turks of the old school, with their long quilted coats of gold or green, almost down to their heels. The narrow eyes, half shut, turned sideways, in the stealthy immobility of the face. Peasants passing you, some of them with fine, unspoilt, wild, mountain faces, stared with a fierce faculty of attention, a dart of eyes which bored into you, screwing their way in with a child's eagerness. They were hurrying homewards, and the streets grew emptier until one came near the bridge, where there was still some movement of men and horses and carriages. As I crossed the bridge, on that difficult footing, the water was still darkened with boats. The opposite shore was one long blaze of lights, and the steep streets of Pera shone confusedly.

IV

Water flows through the city, purifying it; light floods it, making it over again hourly. It lies between the water and the sky, in a great, luxurious abandonment to the light. Seen from the Bosphorus at sunset, Stamboul rises like a great cloud, silhouetted against pure gold, and no more substantial than a cloud; its edges are cut into a pattern of domes and minarets and cypresses, above luminous banks of cloud; it hangs there, lifted and burning, wholly a part of the sky. Around the point of the Seraglio, there is pure sea, with sails and islands; on the right, naked from the sunset the walls and square window-holes of Pera, rising up solidly out of the land.

Sunrise, as I see it from the height of Pera, brings out all the colours of Stamboul, like water washing over veined marble. The whole city, washed by the light, whitens and reddens, every window grows distinct, and the balcony of every minaret. On the water the boats seem to crawl over steel-blue oil. A few thin spires of smoke rise slowly, forming into clouds of sombre fleece above the minarets. The light seems to draw a curtain back slowly over Kassim Pacha; below, the cypresses and half of the valley are still cold.

One morning, looking out before sunrise, I saw a great burning orange moon in the sky. Below, there was a white, woolly, and shining mist over the water, through which I could at first see nothing. The moon had cut a straight and glittering path through the mist, and on this path of light I saw a dark ship, every line of its rigging black and distinct. Gradually, looking into the mist, I saw a few faint shapes, first masts, and then, beyond, houses and domes. The moonlight was over all the valley, luminous with mist; out of which one great tower rose like a lighthouse out of a fairy sea. I turned away, and, coming back to the window a few minutes later, it was day; the moon still shone in the sky, but the light was the cold light of early morning, and in the east a long streak of rose crept up behind the housetops.

Every morning I find a new aspect in the water of the Golden Horn, and in the walls and domes and minarets and cypresses of Stamboul, and along the bare desert line of the horizon, and in the green and brown of the valley and hillside, from Kassim Pacha to the white sprinkled stones of the Jews' cemetery and to the sky. The cypresses below my windows, in the Little Field of the Dead, in whose midst I am living, have their different textures, as the light smooths them to velvet or sharpens the points of their branches.

In the heat of the day, as I sit on a tomb in the Little Field of the Dead, I watch the winding dusty road, with its strings of horses and donkeys, carrying burdens across their backs, roped together in long

tinkling lines; men with burdens, who sit down
among the graves to smoke a cigarette; veiled
women, who pass shrouded from head to feet in
their feredjes, like the dominoes of some players in a
masquerade.   Veiled women, their yashmaks half
lifted, are sitting on a patch of grass outside the
low wooden houses with grated windows, which seem
to grow, huddled, in a cleft of the hillside.   Through
the tops of the cypresses I can catch a broken glitter
of water; beyond, a dome, and three minarets.
Sheep nibble at the short grass, a solemn company
of turkeys goes by, the dogs lie asleep with their
heads against the stones of the road.   There is a
dense, windless heat; not even the dust is alive
enough to move.

On a day of wind, crossing the bridge from
Stamboul about sunset, all is changed.   The water,
darkened by the wind, heaves into little waves,
like the waves of the sea, and the bridge rocks
under one's feet.   Sailing boats are anchored in
the harbour; as the steamers go out and come in,
the thick smoke from their funnels blackens the
air.   I watch the barges, and their difficult passage
under the bridge, the mast lowered as they
pass under; farther out, the small boats rowing
hard against the tide, the rushing six-oared caiques,
the little leaning sails, the foam behind the steamers;
the whole unquiet water, clouded sky, and the pale
gold crescent above the minarets.   Beyond the
bridge, there is a sudden peace, still water, motionless

P

shadows from the stacked masts against the shore; as I go on my way, Pera, rising like a mountain.

At night, as I look from my windows over Kassim Pacha, I never tire of that dull, soft colouring, green and brown, in which the brown of roofs and walls is hardly more than a shading of the green of the trees. There is the lovely curve of the hollow, with its small, square, flat houses of wood; and above, a sharp line of blue-black cypresses on the spine of the hill; then the long, desert plain, with its sandy road, shutting in the horizon. Mists thicken over the valley, and wipe out its colours before the lights begin to glimmer out of it. Below, under my windows, are the cypresses of the Little Field of the Dead, vast, motionless, different every night. Last night each stood clear, tall, apart; to-night they huddle together in the mist, and seem to shudder.

The sunset was brief, and the water has grown dull, like slate. Stamboul fades to a level mass of smoky purple, out of which a few minarets rise black against a grey sky with bands of orange fire. Last night, after a golden sunset, a fog of rusty iron came down, and hung poised over the jagged level of the hill. The whole mass of Stamboul was like black smoke; the water dim grey, a little flushed, and then like pure light, lucid, transparent, every ship and every boat sharply outlined in black on its surface; the boats seemed to crawl like flies on a lighted pane.

V

In this fierce, amazing place, there is always rest by the Sea of Marmora. I liked best to sit on the shore at Yeni-Kapou, where small waves beat on the rocks at my feet, and the masts rocked at anchor close to the shore, or spread their sails against the filmy mountains beyond the islands. The sea glittered placidly along the curve of the decayed port, with its few small ships, and the longer curve going on beyond the Seven Towers, and the cypresses of Kadi-Keui stepping down into the water. Behind, there was the railway, there were a few houses, with great fragments of ruined walls, the ancient sea-walls of the city. A little way along, you came to another, more bustling, line of seashore, almost like Italy; boats bringing in timber, the unloading, the weighing, the loading of donkeys; children, a crowd of dogs, a wooden café in the sea. Beyond the railway lies the mosque of Little Santa Sophia, the sixth-century church of St Sergius and St Bacchus. Whitewash has done all it can to disfigure the lovely interior of a church which is built on the pattern of the church of St Vitale in Ravenna. The mosaics are covered with roughly painted arabesques, the beautiful capitals are white-washed, but the frieze, with its Greek lettering, remains; and the eye, when the mind has helped it to see straight, in spite of the distorted focus of

mihrab and matting, can still recognise the perfect
balance, the lovely proportions, of the structure.

Climb through a few twisting streets, and you
come upon a mosque which I returned to again
and again, for the mere pleasure of being there:
the mosque of Mehmed Pacha, once the church
of St Anastasia. It is set in a nest of trees, on
the edge of the hillside; square-towered doorways,
trailed over with vines, lead into a small square
court, with arcades of trefoil-shaped arches, a simple,
admirably designed fountain in the midst, covered
with a wide wooden roof; thin-leaved trees are
planted around three sides of the court. The
mosque is small and plain, with blue tiles on the
front, and arches of red and white marble. The
walls, on the side overlooking the sea, are covered
with ivy, the only ivy I saw in Constantinople.
Through the barred windows of the outer court
you see thick clusters of trees, with pigeons among
their branches, almost hiding the straight white
wall, and throwing a great black-green shadow on
the terrace beyond. There are a few old and
desolate graves among the grass. As I wandered
to and fro in the courtyard, one or two quiet men
came out of the doors under the arcades, looked
at me quietly, and turned back again without
curiosity.

There is rest by the Sea of Marmora, but
for the Moslem the one harbour of peace, where
he is wholly at home with himself, far from the

mongrel crowds of Pera and Galata and Stamboul, is
the little, fierce, wind-swept suburb of Eyoub, con-
servatively alive among its graves. The Christian
is unwelcome there; and why should he not be
unwelcome? The mosque is the most sacred mosque
in Constantinople, one of the two mosques which
no Christian is allowed to enter; and is there
anything unreasonable in this reticence? It is his
association with other races, his struggle against
the alien forces in his midst, that degrades the
Turk; he learns craft from the Jew and greed
from the Christian. In Eyoub he has drawn
himself aside, he lives the life of his forefathers;
and you find yourself instantly in another atmosphere
as you land from the steamer at the last station on
the Golden Horn. Beyond the water, low hills
rise curved; dark cypresses climb the hillside in
rigid lines; near the shore, rising out of trees, are
the small white dome and the two minarets of the
mosque. The streets are broad, well paved, with
none of the dirt and slime of Constantinople; on
each side of the street are shops in which beads
and rosaries are sold, and you see, for once, really
appetising pancakes being made, clean bread and
clean fruit being sold.˙ Men sit gravely in the
cafés and at the doors of the shops; there is no
noise, no bustle; every eye turns on you, without
approval, but, as you walk quietly through their
midst, without open hostility. The walls around
the mosque are pierced by barred windows, through

which you see bushy trees, and one huge plane-tree, gaping as if from a wound. As I passed, the outer doorway was being repainted, and the black lettering above it was being carefully brightened. The inner court, through which men and women were passing, was well swept; there was none of the dust which lies thick about so many of the mosques; I caught a glimpse of the doorway into the mosque itself: the unadorned white marble was spotlessly white. But a little way beyond the mosque, a winding path begins uphill among the tombs, a kind of stairway with well-swept stairs, between the tombstones; around many of them are iron rails, freshly painted; even the tombs of women, with their flower-topped heads, are sometimes railed round. From the hill top you look down on the Sweet Waters of Europe, a placid lagoon, with its dim water, and pale islands of grasses, and barren shores. Farther to the right, beyond the hill of graves and the mosque, lies the whole curved course of the Golden Horn, with its shores of houses and its many masts, shining under the sunlight. Yet farther to the right are the brown roofs and walls and grated windows of Eyoub, set in masses of green trees, filling the valley, and rising up another hill to the sky. The cypresses around and below swayed in the wind, which came coolingly about one. I sat for a long time on the hill, looking down on this fierce, and, as they call it, fanatical suburb, where I had expected to feel only a sense of peril and discomfort.

Never had these enemies, the Turks, seemed to me
so sympathetic, so reasonable; only, I could not
help feeling that some apology was needed for my
being there at all.

VI

I was standing on the bridge one morning,
looking down into the water, exquisitely blue, in
which the minnows darted like little emerald snakes.
Caiques slid past, almost as swiftly as the minnows;
boats with tall brown masts, all leaning one way,
stood in order against the quay; the sunlight
poured down softly, enveloping the land and water.
I was saying to myself in a kind of dreamy peace
and contentment: how beautiful! when, looking
down at my side, close to the parapet of the bridge,
almost between me and the water, I saw a little girl
lying on the ground; she had drawn up her skirt
and laid it across her legs, in order that she might
show a raw sore which ate into the flesh.

In that contrast all Constantinople is summed up;
and it is that contrast, largely, which makes it so
disturbing, alluring, so violent and seductive at once
in its appeal. It is, as the East is to the West, a
kaleidoscope; but you must be prepared for the
sudden shaking of the colours, and it will be well if
you can look at the picture merely as a picture.
Wherever you go you will hear the clank of a
sword; an officer, a zaptié, passes you; everywhere

there are soldiers prowling, and the soldier here is the scum of the streets, with a ragged uniform as his license to do as he pleases. There are soldiers on guard at every street corner, and outside every public building, in their sentry-boxes of rotten wood, propped up on stones. The man who stops by your side, as you look over the side of the bridge, may be a spy; the merchant from whom you buy in the Bazaar may be told by the police that he is not to sell you books or manuscripts. If anything happens, talk of it as little as you can. One day I saw that a part of the parapet of the bridge had gone; a rope was tied across in its place; and people were looking curiously down into the water. Next day the parapet was in its place again. I asked what had happened. The parapet had given way; fifteen or twenty people had gone over. "Were they drowned?" I asked. I was told not to inquire; the bridge, it was known, wanted mending; no one would mend it; an accident was a kind of natural criticism: nothing must be said about it.

Almost every morning I pass the Sublime Porte. It is a covered doorway of wood and stucco, with a frieze of green lettering, to which the pigeons often add a living frieze with their smooth bodies. Dust and stones are heaped about the Sublime Porte; grass grows between the stones of the courtyard, which rises inside like a mound, paved with cobbles. A fortune-telling woman squats in an angle of the pavement opposite, a negress, with her beads and

charms laid out on a little carpet: the black face
thrust forward out of a veil tightened about it.

One morning, not far from the Sublime Porte, I
met a company of gipsies. Pots and pans, bedding,
all their goods were piled on the backs of donkeys, a
black chicken was tied on the top ; they led dogs in
leash, and all the dogs in the street were barking.
There were several men, and two very handsome
women, one of them a straight-backed old crone
who walked royally. Two little children, as dark
as Hindus, in green and yellow Turkish trousers,
ran behind. The company marched through the
street like an army in the midst of a hostile town.

Just afterwards, near Santa Sophia, I met two
Kurds, with red handkerchiefs about their heads,
and red girdles, who dragged two big bears after
them at the end of long ropes. They had long
poles in their hands, and two tambourines, on which
they beat. The bears snuffled uneasily through the
midst of the dogs, turning nervously at every bark.
They had none of that strange aloofness which I
noticed in the three camels, roped together, which
passed me the other day in one of the streets of
Pera. The dogs barked frantically around them,
but the yellow beasts, with their craning necks and
flat snakes' heads, lounged on indifferently, putting
down their large soft-padded feet with a delicate
choice of the road.

And the dogs, who are in' a sense the masters
here, have their own homelessness in the city which

they have taken for themselves. They look at you without recognition, they have no masters, and they have lost the sense of human relationship. Kindness restores it to them; surprise quickens their gratitude. For the most part they are left alone, and they have made laws for themselves, and taken up their own quarters. They live hardly better than the beggars; they are diseased from birth; and they lie in the streets, as the beggars lie in the streets, with all their sores, sometimes pitied a little, foul, pitiable things. With night they waken into some hideous uneasiness; and their howling, as it comes up through a silence only broken by the tapping of the bekjé's iron staff, is like a sound of loud wind or water far off, waxing and waning, continually going on, and at times, as it comes across the water from Stamboul, like a sound of strings, scraped and plucked savagely by an orchestra of stringed instruments.

VII

Somewhat hidden, under the dust of the city, under the earth itself, or crumbling, a broken wall, a burnt column, the arch of an·aqueduct, there is another older Constantinople, not quite at rest, which looks out on this secret, tragic, spectacular city, the one real thing there. In the At-Meidan there is a hollow pit, railed in with dusty iron

railings; dust, shards, dry plants, fallen stones, a
battered tin pail, lie at the bottom of the pit; and
out of this refuse there rises a broken, headless
column of green bronze, in which three serpents
coil together, like living things.   The head of one
of the serpents is to be seen in the Museum; no
more than the upper jaw, with its flattened head,
ribbed eyes, and little deadly teeth, a thing of
exquisite horror.   Like the coils, it is alive; and
the coils, swelling as they rise out of the pit, seem
to have stiffened suddenly, keeping the outline of
their last palpitation.   The bronze is delicately
frayed; it is coloured as if in some natural vegetable growth.   On one side of the pit is the stone
obelisk of Constantine Poryphyrogenitus, stripped
of its sheath of gilded bronze; on the other side
is the obelisk of rosy granite which Theodosius
brought from Heliopolis: it has still that uncreased
childlike freshness of very aged Egyptian things.
Each commemorates an empire which has come and
passed, but the Serpent Column was old when
Constantine brought it from Delphi, and set it
up in the Hippodrome.   It was cast from the spoils
of the Persians, after the victory of Platæa, and
the names of all the cities which had helped to win
the victory were engraved on its coils: they are not
yet quite erased.   The Christians took it to be a
pagan demon, and a patriarch came by night and
broke off two of its heads.   The Mohammedans
took it to be a Christian idol, and broke off its third

head. Indestructible, it still stands in its place, like a hostile, watchful exile, outlasting many enemies.

Not far off, in the courtyard of a house in a narrow street, there is a trap-door which lifts upon a flight of stone steps, going down into a spacious darkness, paved with water, out of which dim columns rise and recede. By the light of a torch made out of a bunch of tow, one distinguishes the capitals of the columns, admirable in design, alternately plain and carved. The columns are set squarely, twelve feet apart; there are 336 columns; they extend underground as far as Santa Sophia. Built by Constantine in the sixth century, perhaps, as we are told, for a cistern, but rather, as the Turks call it, Yeri-Batan-Serai, a subterranean palace in which the genii of the earth and of the water under the earth might be royally at home, it has a twofold silence, the silence of earthy darkness and the silence of immovable water. To go down into it is like going down into an immeasurable grave, into which all the glory of Byzantium had gone down, living on there, in a ghastly hiding away from life, with the persistence of indestructible things.

Books have been written about the walls of Constantinople, and, as in Rome, it is the walls that still bring the past most solidly into the present. Here, there is no beauty, as in the austere walls of Rome; merely ruined greatness. On one side they go crumbling into the sea, which has not yet

picked their stones to pieces. As you drive round
them on the land, along an unpaved road full of
heaps and hollows, you see a long ragged line of
walls, broken by time, and now yet more desperately
cracking into decay since the earthquake of 1894;
about them, a space of desert land, with great trees
on the borders of deep ditches. The walls are
double, with a moat between wall and wall, bridged
at frequent intervals by square towers. You are
taken to see the little Golden Gate, a mere bricked-
up arch in a wall, but the gap, they say, through
which the Christians are to enter the city, when
they come back to take their own. From the top
of the Seven Towers, on which heads have rotted,
you can see the islands and the whole Sea of
Marmora. You climb through dungeons in which
ambassadors have been imprisoned; you look down
into the pit in which their heads have been thrown.
I saw the names of Venier and Alberti, ambassadors
of Venice, carved on the walls. Everywhere a
palace or a prison had stood, or an enemy had
entered victoriously, or a king had died defending
his city. All the history of the empire is written
in the walls, and can still be read there.

And, around them, the land suffers, scarred with
cruelties; it is hot, thirsty, neglected; it lies like
the dogs, its own master, and left to decay. Dust
lies thick on all the roads, and the roads are all
rocks. Here and there are trees, sometimes ash-
trees, more often cypresses among the tombs. The

way is lined with cemeteries, with their slim stones, embroidered with the decorative Turkish lettering, under the men's turbans or the flower-knobs of the women; some stare gaudily, like Aztec idols. Near the monastery of the miraculous fishes, there is a mad-house, and, as I passed, grave, gentle creatures sat on stone benches, one of them tracing words with his staff in the dust; they looked up sleepily, the curiosity all gone out of their eyes. Inside, through barred windows, I saw a violent face rise up suddenly against the bars, out of the midst of a room full of tumbled beds. An idiot boy begged for pence in the road, and waved his cap at a passing flock of sheep.

VIII

There are no gardens in Constantinople, few open squares, few places set apart for rest; there would be few open squares and places set apart for rest, but for the mosques. The mosque is to the Turk this world and the next, equally. To the Turk every foothold of the earth is sacred, or can become so to his thought, by the mere reverent taking off of his shoes, and turning of his face to the east. The hour of prayer finds him constantly prepared, on whatever soil he may be. Thus his temples are to him so much a part of the world, and of his daily life; he can sleep, transact business there; he requires no images of divine things; his rites are

no more than an invocation of God, and a telling
over to God of his own names of power and mercy.

Courtyard within courtyard, the mosque itself is
a kind of inner court, or patio of heaven.   Its architecture, the dome and minaret, suggests growing
things, the palm tree and the cypress ; and around
it, beyond its first court or *harem*, is a great empty
space, planted around the outer rim with trees, and
surrounded by a stone wall chequered by long rows
of barred windows.   Inside this wall, barbers hang
their brass basins on the trees, and men sit on cane-
bottomed chairs being shaved ; meat and fruit are
sold ; sometimes there is a market, with stalls set
up all over the ground ; the Bajazidié has a living
pavement of pigeons, and the awnings, under which
the merchants of beads and fruits sit with their glass
trays, are covered deep with the droppings and
feathers of the multitude of birds.   Outside the
wall, sometimes under roofs built against it, work
goes on : you hear the hammering of iron, or look
down on a narrow street of rag-shops.   Inside,
though there is buying and selling, and men go
about their daily duties, there is always space for
rest, and there is that religious thing, water.

If you stand in the courtyard of the Suleimanié,
just before the hour of prayer (you have but to
turn, and you can see the water, Galata, and
Scutari, in exquisite fragments) you will see men
coming in one by one, and going up to the washing
place against the wall.   They take off their coats

and shoes, stand on the narrow foothold of stone in front of the tap, and wash hands and feet and head. The carter has tied his horse to a tree; the soldiers stroll in barefoot in their shoes; the many fez shine vividly against the straight white wall. The muezzins are waiting on the minarets; they lean over their balconies; then voice after voice, in the wailing Eastern tone, cries the salutation, one voice striking through another. They move round their balconies, crying to north and south and east and west. The men go in slowly at all the doors, pushing aside the heavy curtain.

It is this mosque, which is set on the highest hill, and seems to crown the city, that Turkish poets have called "splendour" and "joy." And indeed, seen from the outside, it is the most beautiful mosque in Constantinople. Its admirable proportions, its severe and elegant bulk, its whole mass and height, stand out square and grey and uprising against the blue of the sky; a great grey building, with its flat surfaces, like the walls of a vast house, and great doorways, level with the wall, squared round by barred windows, and the long square lines of the *harem*, four five-sided minarets rising from its corners, with their elaborately carved balconies, hung with little black-lamps.

Nietzsche has said of Christian churches that they are like caverns, with clammy odours, in which the free soul cannot rise to its full height. The mosque is spacious, empty for God and man, arched

with a great dome, like the earth itself; and it is
open to all, a place where men may continue their
daily lives, in which adoration becomes a part of
the day's doings; and the birds make their home
there, and fly in and out of the windows under the
dome; you hear the clatter of their wings, and see
their shadow on the floor as they pass.   The interior
of Santa Sophia, disfigured as it is by paint, and
stripped of ornament, is like an airy house of prayer,
and, gradually, one comes to feel singularly at home
with its height and depth.   The great dome floats
in the air, seeming scarcely to touch the half-domes
out of which it rises, and the effect of this hollowing
out of the air, so to speak, rather than of building
against it, gives one a singular impression: I never
felt so much inside anything, and yet so solidly
on the ground.   This church of the divine wisdom
brings you serenity, not awe; it liberates, does not
overwhelm.   Its religious appeal is abstract, not in
the cold, reasoning way of Cologne Cathedral, but
in a universal way of its own.   Any religion could
worship the principle of wisdom within its walls,
which have needed no more than a few inches'
change of focus to pass from the Greek to the
Moslem faith.   Its structure leaves it free for the
occupation of God himself, limiting him to no form
of his divine essence.

   The interior of Santa Sophia is the most beautiful
interior in Constantinople, just as the exterior of
the Suleimanié is the most beautiful exterior.   This

Byzantine church, which set the pattern to the
later builders of mosques, though it once contained
many beautiful things which have been taken away
fiom it, and though it has lost the better part of
the glory of its mosaics, crudely painted over by
the piety of the Turks, has lost, after all, little.
Its genius is the genius of structure; what remains
of the decoration is no more than a delicate veiling
of that vast, rhythmical idea in stone. There is
still, though dimmed, the gold of the dome, which
glows as the sun enters by the little windows
around its base; with, under the arches which
support the gallery, bits of gold sky, as in St
Mark's, but less marvellous; glimpses of bright
mosaic in small arches high up; the black marble
and mother-of-pearl under the upper arches of the
gallery; the capitals and the carving above them,
like Valenciennes lace. There are the porphyry
columns from the Syrian Temple of the Sun, and
the slabs of marble let into the walls, like Japanese
pictures, each with its faint indication of form in
a single delicately shaded veining of colour. And
there are the few additions of the Turks: the
mihrab, the carved stone pulpit with its two banners,
the two dim and lovely carpets, on which Mahomet
is thought to have prayed, hung on the walls, the
four immense green discs of wood, on which a
fine artist in the writing of letters has painted in
gold the names of God and of his prophets. And,
in its corner, there is the invariable grandfather's

clock, striking the Eastern hours, by which the hours of prayer are regulated in all the mosques.

As the hour of prayer comes round, the nasal voices of the young students who sway to and fro, reciting the Koran, are silent; men in the red fez, carrying their shoes in their hands, steal in from all sides, ranging themselves in rows along the strips of matting which cover the floor; a cry is heard from the roof of the mastaba, a sort of flat roof on pillars, on which the ulemas, or priests, are stationed; there is an intoning, very like the intoning in a Catholic church, a salutation of God, repeated over and over As one looks down from above, one sees row after row of bare or stockinged feet, as the worshippers sit cross-legged, holding their hands out, with the palms turned upwards; then all rise to their feet, then kneel, then touch the ground with their fore- heads; the sonorous voices, carried into echoing heights by the vaults, curiously muted as the faces bend over. There is a profound simplicity and solemnity in this worship without elaborate rites, this direct intercourse with God; in these formal, conventional Eastern prostrations, the cry of the muezzin from the minaret, the cry of the ulema from the mastaba.

IX

The dervishes are the monks of the East. They live apart, in tekkés or monasteries, and wear a

singular monastic costume of their own. The
turning dervishes and the howling dervishes have
each their ceremonies, and these are really religious
ceremonies, not meant for the public at all, although
they are content to make a little money from the
visits of curious strangers. They have several
tekkés in Constantinople, and their ceremonies can
be attended at fixed hours on certain days of the
week. I saw the Mevlevi, or turning dervishes, at
the tekké of the Grande Rue de Péra, and the
Rufai, or howling dervishes, at Scutari in Asia.

The tekké of the Grande Rue de Péra is a little,
broken-down mosque in the corner of a dingy
courtyard. The inside is like the inside of a Paris
dancing-hall: in the middle there is a polished
wooden floor, and this is surrounded by a low rail,
with wooden pillars supporting a small gallery.
The people stand crowded together all round the
hall, on the outer side of the rail; a few foreigners
pay for seats in the gallery, and in their midst, but
shut off from them in a sort of central room, are
the musicians, who play on long reedy flutes, giving
a very soft note, and on two little drums, held in
men's laps, and beaten with tiny drumsticks.
Opposite the musicians, but on the lower floor, is
the mihrab, and the imaam, or ·prior, stands or sits
on a strip of carpet with his back to the mihrab.
The dervishes stand motionless around the inner
space, with bent heads and arms crossed; they
wear long cloaks, of dull colours, drab, green, and

brown, and on their heads tall, earthy caps, like elongated fez. The music plays continuously, and one or two of the musicians sing in high-pitched voices. The drums tap out the beat, and the flutes breathe softly round the notes, while the voices seem to come in irregularly, cutting through them, or going against them, but always guided, like an improvisation, by the inexorable beat.

At a signal from the music the dervishes began to walk slowly round and round ; each, as he came to the mihrab, paused, turned, and bowed low to the dervish following him, who in turn bowed low to him, took his place, turned, and repeated the same action. The movements were slow, deliberate, ceremonious. When all had revolved back into their stations in the circle, the music changed, and the dervishes dropped their cloaks, and stood motionless for a moment in their long white gowns, white drawers, and bare feet. Then, slowly, one after another clasped his hands about his shoulders, and began to turn. As he turned he seemed to unwind himself, and his arms slowly straightened out, and so remained, the palm of the right hand turned up, the palm of the left hand turned down. Soon all were turning, at different rates of speed, but in obedience to the fixed beat of the drums. They turned at the outer edge of the floor, in a circle, each turning from right to left ; and gradually, but very slowly, the whole circle moved round the floor. The gentle, sleepy music went on, and as the white cloaks of the dervishes lifted and stood out around them in the wind of the movement, it seemed as if great white bells spun monotonously, with a kind of low, hissing creak, as the bare heels turned, sweating, on the floor.

The music quickened or slackened, and the dervishes kept time, each at his own rate of speed. There was a short, black-bearded man who whirled like a teetotum; another, a tall old man, with closed eyes, turned with a slow and dreamy movement, as a snake, standing on its tail, might curve itself painfully and delicately round. There was a little boy of about twelve, who turned with all a child's seriousness; few seemed to move mechanically, or as if the movement had not some secret meaning. Suddenly the music stopped, the dervishes went back to their places, put on their cloaks, and sat down on the floor; there was some chanting, a prayer, and an old man stood up and recited something out of the Koran; then the turning began again, but for a much shorter space of time. At the end, each dervish went up to the imaam, who stood with his back to the mihrab, kissed his hand, laid his head on his shoulder, as if kissing his cheek, and then, passing on, grasped the hand of the dervish next to him, laying his head for an instant on his shoulder, and passing on, in a strange and stealthy rhythm, always in circles and half-circles, within the one continually turning circle which moved round the floor. The whole ceremony was made out of the rhythm of circles, and was, I doubt not, a ritual for the attainment of ecstasy by some vertigo of the soul and the senses, which might well swoon into a kind of circling immobility.

In the ceremonies of the turning dervishes, there is beauty, together with a gentle hallucination which seems to draw one slowly into its own circle. The ecstasy is that of an enveloping dream, into which one sinks delightedly. But the ecstasy of the howling dervishes is a form of delirium, by which one may reach, first, imbecility, and then an epileptic madness. I went over to Asia to see them, across the Bosphorus, to the Asiatic suburb of Constantinople. Scutari is built like an amphitheatre on the slope of Mount Boulgourlou, a rocky and dusty height from which you look down on the Bosphorus, and on the Sea of Marmora, and on the Black Sea. This almost wholly Oriental town is fierce and primitive, with unpaved and precipitous streets, which lead upward from the thronged and tumultuous landing-place to the great cemetery on the hill. The soil is sacred, and the tombs crowd upon one another in the midst of a forest of cypresses. Almost at its feet is the tekké of the dervishes, a plain wooden building surrounded by a courtyard. As one enters the courtyard there is a smell of incense; óne catches a glimpse, through a side-door, of men moving on some priestly business, and, through an open window, of coffins laid one above another. Inside, it is a small, square hall;

the centre of the floor is railed round, and a low platform stands in one corner, near the door by which the dervishes go in and out. The ceiling, with its wooden beams, is painted green, the balustrades and corner pillars are of unpainted wood, but with touches of green paint; the walls are green, and the mihrab is a deeper green. The mihrab is hung with knives and chains and with all manner of instruments of torture, used by the dervishes when they cut themselves in the frantic rites of the Bairam. On each side an old flag of beautiful workmanship is stretched out; texts from the Koran, in gilt frames, are hung upon the walls, and between them are rows of tambourines of different sizes, set close together. The floor is covered with mats, and, as I entered, I saw the dervishes seated on them in a long row, opposite the mihrab; a few priests sat at right angles to them, in the middle of the floor; a gold incense-burner smoked at the feet of the imaam, who sat in the curve of the mihrab. The imaam was dressed in black; he was small, with delicate features, black hair and beard, profound eyes, and exquisite hands. He sat there like an idol, waving his hands slowly outwards and upwards and downwards, as if making hypnotic passes, and swaying very gently. He chanted in a low clear voice, and the chant was taken up by the priests in the middle, and passed on to the row of dervishes, who responded in a hoarse chorus as they swayed to and fro with a steady motion. One of the priests had precisely the face of Rabelais, with brutal, magnetising eyes, and a sardonic laughter grinning from his mouth.

The swaying, and the guttural cry: "Allah hou! Allah hou!" began slowly. The dervishes swayed backwards and forwards, and then with a circular and sidelong movement, and the force of the movement increased gradually, and the voices gradually deepened. At last they rose to their feet, each man laid his hand on the shoulder of his neighbour, and, thus linked into a flexible chain, they swayed all together, and the force of the movement and the energy of the deep cry increased and quickened. There was a movement to the right, then to the left, and a stamp of the bare heel, as each man seemed to hurl his body as far as it would go without losing foothold, and then hurl it back again with a kind of semi-circular swing of the hips. The whole line swayed together, with exactly the same general movement, but, as with the turning dervishes, each man had his own way of moving: a pale, bull-necked young man worked violently, painfully, with every muscle, and an old lean man bent and doubled like a piece of indiarubber. The swaying went on without a pause, and the dervishes closed their eyes, and cried with hoarse beast-like cries, and seemed to relapse into a fierce and stolid dizziness, while the imaam, watching them with his controlling eyes, and guiding them with his thrilling voice and delicate hands, moved to and fro, always master of himself and of them, setting the rhythm of the movement.

After the ceremony had gone on for some time, a gigantic negro, seven feet high, came out of the inner room, and took up his place in the midst of the other dervishes. For a little while he could not catch the rhythm; then he found it, gave himself up to it, and then came the most horrible thing I have ever seen. The negro swayed with the whole force of his huge bulk, battering the air with his head, which he hurled this way and that way; with every movement the head rolled round on his shoulders, and as I stood behind him I saw a convulsed face, with closed eyes and open mouth, appear and disappear, a mass of bloodshot and sweating blackness, with the glittering white of the teeth and the pink of the inside of the mouth. He howled like a wild beast in agony, he gave great gasps that seemed to shatter his body; at every moment I expected to see him roll over on the floor in an epileptic fit.

Meanwhile the movement had grown quicker, more rigid, more automatic; and the savage howl of the chant had sunk into an almost inarticulate "hou! hou!" A priest went along the line of now almost unconscious swaying figures, and took off the outer cap from each man's head, leaving a white linen skull-cap. A baby was brought in and carried close under the swaying heads, that some healing might come to it from the breath

and sweat of their hysteria. Men and children
lay down on the ground, and the imaam walked
on them, in soft yellow leather slippers, drawing
his feet along the body where it was sick, and
stooping and blowing on it, and laying his hand
on men's shoulders while he looked into their faces
and breathed on them. The imaam had the face
of a saint, with wise, profound, gentle, and imperious
eyes; and I am sure he believed in his power, his
mission. When he trod on men and children,
stooped over them, breathed upon them, he seemed
to feel that a force was passing out of him into
them; and certainly he had the dervishes in his
hand, as if they were wild beasts, and he their
keeper. And there was a hardness under the
gentleness, which meant the controlling mind. He
led them, shared in the impulse which he had
evoked, but never abandoned himself to it. Are
these epileptics led by a true mystic? And have
they whirled and cried themselves into an ecstasy,
out of which, as the people think, there can come
messages, and a gift of healing?

There is contagion in it, and the brain reels, and
the body is almost swept into the orgy. This
motion of swaying is the Eastern lullaby for the
senses; it is one of the gestures of meditation,
and the student sways as he recites the Koran.
In the howling dervishes I felt the ultimate, because
the most animal, the most irrational, the most insane,
form of Eastern ecstasy. Nothing I have ever seen

has given me such an impression of witchcraft. One might have been in Central Africa, or in some Saturnalia of barbarians. Inhuman, savage, incalculable, a frenzy and yet a part of religion, I seemed to find in it the essence of this strange place, in which the mind does not exist, in which reason is forgotten, and the senses are petted like slaves that have become masters, and have been masters so long that the people have forgotten that they were ever slaves.

X

The Sultan lives on the outskirts of Constantinople, in the modern Yildiz Kiosque, rather a great villa than a palace; he lives there, as the Pope lives in the Vatican, a sort of prisoner by choice. Once every week, on Friday, he drives some three hundred yards from his palace-gates to the door of the mosque of Hamidié, attends prayers there, as official head of the church, and then drives back again, in another carriage. The first carriage is lined with blue satin, the second carriage is drawn by two white horses, and the reins are laced with solid gold. Regiments of soldiers line the way, court officials in gold lace surround the carriage, walking down the hill, when the Sultan drives slowly, and running up the hill, when he drives fast; and the Sultan is seen by no more than a handful of invited guests, in the

Ambassadors' pavilion and on the terrace below.   If
you are in the Ambassadors' pavilion, you are advised
not to lean out too noticeably from the windows ; if
you are on the terrace below, you are watched closely
by a bevy of agents in plain clothes, who, as the
Sultan is about to pass, step in front of you.   When
the carriage reaches the door of the mosque, the
Grand Vizier gets out backwards, and the court
officials crowd up the steps after the Sultan, like a
body-guard.

The situation and the spectacle are alike worthy
of the Cæsars, and there is about them the same
celestial irony.   Not even in Rome was there a
finer stage for such a spectacle than this hill, from
which you look across roofs to the Bosphorus.
And the spectacle has a splendour almost wholly
barbaric; opulent, unchecked, with its unconscious
naïvetés.   I went early, not wishing to miss any
significant detail.   After a little waiting, I saw a
stir begin far off, and then, around the hill, came
troopers on grey and white horses, carrying lances
with crimson pennons; after them, troopers on
brown horses; then infantry dressed in white;
then the Syrian guards in electric blue, with green
turbans rolled round their fez ; then more foot
soldiers, first in brown, then in dull blue.   The
soldiers formed in line across all the avenues leading
to the mosque.   A group of women with veiled
heads stood just beyond them, and, beyond these,
people moved to and fro.   Suddenly the line opened,

and there was a rush of tiny carts filled with sand, followed by men with spades, who emptied the sand, and by men with brooms, who spread it equably over the sloping ground from the gates of the mosque to the gates of the palace. Meanwhile, cabs were driving up, and men in gold lace got out of them, followed by servants carrying Gladstone bags; then a few priests, also followed by servants carrying Gladstone bags. Black eunuchs, dressed like clergymen, in frock-coats, went to and fro, all immensely tall and thin, with pained and hideous faces, and a shambling stride. An old one-eyed man, nearly black-skinned, and black with filth, in the green turban of the hadji, went about with a blackened sheepskin water-bottle and a brass bowl, and poured out water for the soldiers. The soldiers had all taken their places, striding up the hill with that singular step, like the step of wild animals, the leg thrown forward sharply, and set down on the toe, the knee doubling inwards at every step. They stood there, mass after mass of barbaric colour, waiting expectantly. Presently the Sultan's sons, children and young men, with whitened faces, rode down the hill, and halted their horses; three closed carriages came slowly out of the palace-gates; as they passed, one caught a glimpse, through the windows, of the silks and satins of Paris gowns, of white gloves with rings outside, of faces veiled to the eyes. The carriages entered the gates of the mosque, turned a little aside, and the horses were unharnessed. Almost at the last moment a butcher's cart dashed through the midst of the soldiers, up the path prepared for the Sultan, and in at the palace gates. No one took any notice of it.

The clock struck, the muezzin cried from the minaret; there was a sound of bugles and a guttural shout from the soldiers, as the Sultan appeared, driving slowly. The Grand Vizier, a very fat man, sat with his back to the horses. One saw the keen, dark, restless face of the Sultan, full of brooding anxiety; the fez, the frock-coat buttoned to the chin, the dark grey military overcoat. With his courtiers before him and behind him, he drove at walking pace through the ranks of the soldiers, a small, frail being, who sat cold and anxious in the midst of all this magnificence of homage to his supreme power. Afterwards, in the palace, as one spoke with him through an interpreter, noticing his attentive courtesy, his watchful scrutiny of the faces before him, one saw perhaps the least to be envied of the kings of the earth, in this small dark stealthy man, with manners of frightened and threatening gentleness, who stepped softly to and fro, in his military overcoat, with his hand on his sword.

XI

Women have no souls, say the Turks. Well, Turkish women have none. The soul in them sleeps, and without dreams. Their eyes are like lustrous oil, and shine without individual fire. Their eyes are like the conscious eyes of animals that have been taught coquetry; they have instinct and artifice, and nothing between. They grow sleek in captivity, and, not being wholly human, they paint their faces and dye their nails and their hair, that they may be more decorative than humanity. Their faces have the precise, not quite perfect, regularity of early painting and sculpture, in which men trimmed nature, a little awkwardly. The nose is apt to be too long or too prominent, the chin too thickened. The mind has done nothing to model the lines of their faces finely; the lines are always in smooth curves, in which elegance sleeps. Beauty, in them, is an exterior thing, into which the individuality does not enter. They are as they were made in the beginning; they change only to fatten and to fade; they die children whom life has taught nothing but the taste of sweet and bitter.

In a book of Arab love-poetry which I have been reading in a French translation, I find that it is always for their languor that the poet of the East praises the eyes of a woman. "Creature with languid eyes," begins one poem; "her eyes slay by their lascivious weakness more surely than sharp swords," says another; "in your glances there floats an intoxicating languor which makes me drunk," says another. There is something of this quality in all the beautiful Turkish eyes that I have seen; often it is their only beauty, and to the Turk that beauty is sufficient. It is asleep, and it is for him to awaken it, and it is to awaken only for his pleasure.

The Turk, man as well as woman, is still unawakened; the mind, here, does not exist; there is only the animal and its instinct. The people, their cloistered women, and their homeless dogs in possession, are all alike creatures of instinct. They do not reason; they make arbitrary rules; and then fight or submit. Hence their massacres, and the too hasty logic of them; hence that helpless complication of their money, by which you have to buy change, and cheat or be cheated every time. There is no right or wrong side of the road; every one tries to push his own way through the crowd, regardless of every one else, and unable to realise that a little forbearance on the part of each would ease the way of all. This is the blind side of fatalism, with its otherwise finely tragic acceptance of things. The dogs, like the people, are fatalists. I saw one day a dog whose paw had been trodden on; he barked in protesting pain, and looked pathetically at the boy who had hurt him: the boy lifted his heel significantly, and the dog merely turned quietly away.

R

The Turk has no pity, and it is pity which civilises. There is a speech in Mr Bridges' play, "The Christian Captives," which says, more precisely than I can say it, just what one is conscious of in the mental limitations of the Turk:

> " Now I see
> Nature hath vainly lavished on these Moors
> Bravery and beauty and all gifts of pride ;
> And left them barbarous for lack of thee,
> Sweet Pity, of human sorrow born : 'tis thou
> Dost raise man 'bove the brutes : 'tis thou dost make
> His heart so singular, that he alone,
> Himself commiserating, against heaven
> Pushes complaint, and finds within his heart
> Room for all creatures, that like him are born
> To suffer and perish."

The Turk has learnt neither wisdom nor revolt through pity. He gives to the beggar, and he lets the dog take, because it is a usage sanctioned by his religion ; he fulfils it with a certain disdain. Does he not treat the dog and the Christian with the same not unkind contempt? He does not willingly touch either. Against Heaven he pushes no complaint, no matter what may befall him ; he has his formula: "It is as God wills." Ask him if he expects fine weather to-morrow, he answers: " Please God ; " and he will answer nothing else. He refuses to admit connection between cause and effect, as he refuses to acknowledge beauty except as a part of antiquity. One day in Santa Sophia, a ulema, who had been standing near me, watching me with a suspicion which gradually melted into a kind of sympathy, as I sat on the floor looking up at the dome and looking around at the walls, said to me with a gesture of satisfaction, in the one word which he could use to express his meaning: " Antique!" That word in Turkish, " eski," is the most approving of all words: it means that a thing is old, coming down from one's forefathers, and therefore has come to be a synonym for what is beautiful, in artistic matters.

XII

The attraction of the East for the West is after all nostalgia; it is as if, when we are awakened by dreams, we remember that forgotten country out of which we came. We came out of the East, and we return to the East; all our civilisation has been but an attempt at forgetting, and, in spite of that long attempt, we still remember. When we first approach it, the East seems nothing more than one great enigma, presented to us almost on the terrifying terms of the Sphinx. We are on the threshold of a mystery, a curtain trembles over some veiled image, perhaps the image of wisdom. The grave faces of worshippers look into our faces without curiosity; they come out into the light from behind the veil and go about their daily business, and they are as inscrutable to us as if really they were in

communion with a wisdom which we do not know.
Perhaps, after all, this secret with which they seem
to go about is no more than certain ordinary and
of necessity incommunicable thoughts.   Here everything is incommunicable ; there is a barrier between
us and them, as narrow perhaps and as real as the
barrier between Europe and Asia : you have only
to cross the Bosphorus.

The   true   East,   one   imagines,   might   come
ultimately to have its satisfaction for us, if only
in our admiration before a complete, finished thing
which we may not understand.   In Constantinople,
we meet the East half-way ; it has all the finished
barbarism of the West in conflict with its own
fiercer elements.   In that still hostile corner of
Europe, the East still has to fight for foothold ; it
has never been let alone long enough to give itself
up to its own leisure.   Left to himself, the Turk's
finest capacity is for an ironical repose, as he sits
aside while the world goes by.   He has settled
now into a tragic, not satisfied, unstirred immobility ;
he desires no change, but things as they are do
not give him happiness.   Under his acceptance of
them he has a few fierce ideas, held like swords.
Religion which becomes fanaticism ; fatalism which
becomes inertia ; pride which becomes a mask for
ignorance, guide or station him.   In his rejection
of the West he has not been able to keep the
West out of his city, and the West is beginning to
soak into his soul.

To the stranger in Constantinople, this fierce and enigmatical East, made fiercer and more enigmatical by the West, comes with a kind of repulsion and attraction at once. It hurts you, and then it enchants you, and then as it enchants you more it hurts you more, and you succumb to it, and struggle against it, and are gripped by all its tentacles; and if you break away from it you leave something of yourself behind with it. People live there hating it and unable to leave it. Its attraction is like the attraction of those women whom it is impossible to live with or without; and what is subtlest in its power to attract is precisely that sense of a revulsion turned violently back upon itself.

AUTUMN, 1902.

CPSIA information can be obtained
at www.ICGtesting.com
Printed in the USA
BVHW072253130223
658299BV00016B/729

9 781113 191298